JAMAICANS IN NOTTINGHAM

Narratives and Reflections

Norma Gregory

Norma Gregory
3/7/15

H
HANSIB

First published in 2015
by Hansib Publications Limited

Reprinted 2015

P.O. Box 226, Hertford, Hertfordshire, SG14 3WY
United Kingdom
Email: info@hansibpublications.com

www.hansibpublications.com

ISBN 978-1-910553-01-5

A CIP catalogue record for this book
is available from the British Library.

Production
Hansib Publications Limited

Printed in Great Britain.

DEDICATION

To those who have courage to seek,
to those who find resilience to stand through struggle,
and to those who pass the baton to the next generation.
Thank you.
N.J.G.

ACKNOWLEDGEMENTS

It must be said here that the sourcing and collation of material for this publication could not have come to fruition in isolation and without the time, kindness and generosity of many people. Therefore, a massive show of gratitude stated here is for all interviewees and contributors who were willing and courageous enough to share their unique life stories with the world.

Firstly, a very big thank you goes to Mr Pitman Browne to whom I will be forever grateful, for his instrumental input editing and proofreading this work and for his positive feedback and encouragement throughout the completion of this book. He has provided valuable guidance with considered accuracy and detailing that would not have been possible to achieve in his absence.

A special thanks goes to: staff at the Nottingham News Centre CIC, the ACNA Centre and its members, the Marcus Garvey Centre, Tuntum Housing Association, Nottinghamshire Archives, Mojatu, Nottingham University, New Art Exchange, Nottingham Trent University, Nottingham City Council, Communities Inc., Nottinghamshire County Council and individuals who have gone that extra mile through their continual assistance and support namely:

Merlita Bryan, Arnold 'Kwame' Wright, Trevor Howell, Des Wilson, Reverend Eve Pitts, Reverend Sean Samuel, Reverend Pat Bailey, Michael Henry, Richard Renwick, Chris Weir, Des Powe, Delroy Brown, Veronica Barnes, Professor Cecile Wright, Joseph 'Rodney' James, Massimiliano Caldini, Rosanna Ottewell, Lillieth 'Fay' Wade, Jean Wallace, Ann Hasler, Charles Sagoe, Dionne Rose, Rose Thompson, Lena Gregory, Verna Gregory, Celia Gregory, Flona Myers, Bryan O'Connor, Olivia O'Connor, family, friends and many others whom have been a source of encouragement over the years to support the completion of this book.

Thank you and baracka (Kiswahili, 'blessings').

IMAGE CREDITS

The publisher and author would like to thank the following individuals and organisations for access and permissions for use of images:

Nottingham News Centre, Nottingham City Council, Pitman Browne, Bob Wallace PYKCHA, Keith Steele Photography, Tuntum Housing Association, George Powe & Jill Westby Archives, Lena Gregory, Calvin Wallace, Consetta Whiteley, Joe 'Rodney' James, William Stewart, Kate Hayward, Stephen McLaughlin, Michael Edwards, Ray Gale, Charles Sagoe, Jane and Western Vaccianna, ACNA Centre, Nottinghamshire Archives, Nottingham Evening Post, Nottingham Journal, Nottingham Evening News, Nottinghamshire Guardian and Mining Heritage. Every effort has been taken to locate permissions for images included. Copyright remains with the creator.

FRONT COVER IMAGES CREDITS

Top row (from left):
Jamaicans and friends at the Nottingham Council House, 2012 celebrating Jamaica's 50th Year of Independence.

Photo: Michael Edwards. Courtesy of Nottingham City Council

Gregory family, Christmas time, living at 3 Bedford Walk, the Hyson Green Flats, 1975.

Courtesy of Lena Gregory Archives

Right column (from top):
Pitman Browne (left), Milton Crosdale (third left) and friends of the West Indian Students' Association, 1968.

Courtesy of Pitman Browne Archives

Flona, Norma and Verna Gregory, 1973.

Photo by Mr Brown. Courtesy of Lena Gregory Archives

George Leigh (left) and friends at the Astoria Ballroom, 1958.

Courtesy of Kate Hayward Archives

Bottom row (from left):

Lee Arbouin, Jamaican and Nottingham author and
community development pioneer.

Photo: courtesy of Nottingham News Centre

Merlita Bryan welcomes Dr Julius Garvey, son the
late Honourable Marcus Garvey to Nottingham, 2013.

Photo: courtesy of Nottingham News Centre

Desmond Wilson, as Lord Mayor of Nottingham
(2003-2003 and 2005-2006).

Photo: courtesy of Nottingham City Council

The official opening of the Nottingham Caribbean
Carnival, 2013 by the Lord Mayor of Nottingham
Cllr Merlita Bryan.   Photo: courtesy of Nottingham News Centre

For further information contact:
www.nottinghamnewscentre.com
info@nottinghamnewscentre.com

CONTENTS

PREFACE

Jamaicans in Nottingham: Narratives and Reflections is a collection of autobiographies, interviews and articles forming narratives and personal reflections that chart the private and public lives of many Jamaicans who have made a massive difference in Nottingham and Nottinghamshire, over the last sixty years or so.

This book joins a merging cohort of Black British, non-fiction literature that forms part of an under-researched area in the history of Nottingham people and British, Caribbean and African history in general.

This book constitutes a selection of true narratives from a selection of first and second generation Jamaicans, post World War II Jamaican migrants and Jamaican / British nationals. There was an estimated 2,500 West Indians (mainly from Jamaica, Trinidad, St Kitts, British Guiana and other Islands) living in Nottingham in 1958, with the 1951 UK Census suggesting that there were 2, 024 Jamaicans in Nottingham and in the 1911 Census 9, 189 African and Caribbean people (32% of the national figures for people of African and Caribbean descent) living in London.

Therefore, the essence of this book is to share with the readers, the experiences of many hard working, resilient Jamaican people in Nottingham. Thus, this book aims to give a faithful and accurate portrayal of these personal narratives told to me in the quiet of their homes and work places. All the interviews were recorded, transcribed and interpreted into coherent and fascinating texts for this book that make up a patchwork of life stories, giving a picture of rich experiences, of both challenges and achievements in Nottingham.

Jamaicans in Nottingham: Narrative and Reflections aims to give a valuable overview from individuals who have contributed to the social, cultural and economic life of the city of Nottingham. There are many more to be interviewed as this book does not cover the entire scope of Jamaicans in Nottingham due to resources available. However, with additional time, resources and wider support, further volumes could be compiled in the future. All things are possible!

REASONS FOR WRITING THIS BOOK

As an individual hailing from African Caribbean heritage and born in Nottingham, UK, I have always felt the need to assist in documenting life, 'as it was and as it is' for future generations to access through print or online media.

I felt the need to help document narratives and oral reflections of challenges and achievements for future generations to read or to use as a research resource as well as a way of maintaining links with my African Caribbean cultural heritage. I wanted to capture *real stories*, from a variety of Jamaicans, from all walks of life, born or residing in Nottingham from the late 1940s to the present day. This book is a testament to them.

I believe that understanding and learning from pioneers is crucial for the social, economic and mental strength needed to grow and develop in the world we live so we can adapt, successfully within a climate adduced to positive and negative global changes. Inclusion, equality and 'voice' are elements that I promote and invest in, which I hope permeates this work.

I have sourced this collection of narratives and oral reflections from Jamaicans in Nottingham over a period of three years by way of meetings and recordings (through Dictaphone and written notes), then spent many hours (if not months) transcribing their answers from Journalistic style questions. I wrote up the extensive transcripts in a style that maintains a true sense of tone and authenticity, in simple Standard English, (and some use of Jamaican patois to illustrate expression) that is easy to understand and accessible to both the elderly and the younger generations. I have spent time to include many photographs, images and relevant newspaper cuttings in the hope of presenting a worthy and interesting, visual and vibrant book. *Enjoy!*

N.J.G

FOREWORD

COUNCILLOR MERLITA BRYAN,
FORMER LORD MAYOR OF NOTTINGHAM (2013-2014)

Jamaicans have been making a massive impact on the social, economic, scientific, historical, cultural, musical, political, religious, sporting and educational life of Nottingham and Nottinghamshire over several decades and it is now a well-known fact that people of African heritage have been living and contributing to life in the UK for centuries, if not thousands of years.

Added to this bastion of influence, is a grand collection of voices, articulated within these pages, to help illustrate the point I am making. The narration of all these heart-felt experiences could never have come at a better time than that of coinciding with the momentous milestone of the 53rd Year of Jamaica's Independence in August 2015.

Jamaicans in Nottingham: Narratives and Reflections intends to be a record of memories and reflections charting the private and public lives of many Jamaicans who have made a massive difference, ultimately through survival and resilience. According to the 1951 Census, there was an estimated total of 2,024 Jamaicans in Nottingham, UK. Currently, there is an estimated 2.7 million native Jamaicans,

with an estimated 150,000 in the UK and 4% in Nottingham alone. These figures suggest that from a relatively small cohort of people, much of credit has been produced by Jamaicans, over centuries and in particular in Nottingham, over the last sixty years or so. They have helped to shape the community of Nottingham, through various methods, for the better, which we can read about in this thoughtful publication.

Many Jamaicans have affected numerous other communities, on a wider scale, through professional and personal achievements. My role as Lord Mayor of Nottingham from 2013 to 2014 is proof enough that changes can and will come.

Enjoy the personal narratives and reflections brought together in this publication, and take positive action in your community today. The time is right, once again, to embrace our rich heritage as African Caribbean people, particularly those born or living in Nottingham and across the UK. Let us build on the significant work we have started in order to improve equality and inclusion for all.

Merlita Bryan undertaking official duties as Lord Mayor of Nottingham 2013-2014. Photo: Nottingham News Centre

SECTION 1

JAMAICANS IN NOTTINGHAM

A Collection of Narratives and Reflections of the Past

CHAPTER 1

REFLECTIONS FROM GEORGE POWE
WORLD WAR II VETERAN AND COMMUNITY CAMPAIGNER

My name is Oswald George Powe and I was born on the 11th August 1926 in Kingston, Jamaica and I am of Chinese African descent. During the latter part of 1943, I arrived in the U.K. aged seventeen, not knowing I would become a resident of this country for over sixty-nine years. After leaving high school in Jamaica in January 1943, I joined the Royal Air Force where I was taught a history of the British Empire as the ethos of British culture had already been entrenched in our education system.

There were adverts and posters for men to join the armed forces so I applied. A lot of young people wanted to fight for their 'mother country' but in my opinion, this did not detract from the notion that people knew they were being oppressed. This I believe is one of the contradictions created through colonialism.

A Jamaican called Roger May wrote articles in Jamaica during the 1940s, advising Jamaicans not to join the British armed forces. He was arrested for sedition because of his beliefs.

Fighting fit: Oswald George Powe aged 17 joins the Royal Air Force in 1943.

Photo: Courtesy of George Powe and Jill Westby Archives

A SOLDIER'S LIFE

I came to England on a troop ship called the *Arbiter*. This ship was converted to carry a maximum number of troops and was fitted with sling hammocks, which we had to pull down in the morning into 'mess decks'. Each compartment had six hammocks and some table facilities. Sometimes we ran short of food on the journey. Everything was not always simple and comfortable as sometimes the ship had to move away and quickly change course to avoid being entangled in submarine nets, which could be dangerous for all on board.

We sailed from Jamaica to America, Iceland and then on to England. The journey lasted seventeen days from America to England. In the military, during war time, we were not told anything about our route or the journey.

All I had with me was my issued gun. I carried no suitcase as we were not allowed to wear civilian clothing: only clothing that was issued to us. It was not until 1948 that particular civilian items were allowed. I remember wearing a pair of black, thick rubber soled shoes. These lasted five years.

I was stationed in Kent where I earned six shillings a week before being moved to a military camp in Yorkshire. We were taught to use firearms as well as the opportunity to learn elements of a trade. The armed forces never gave you a complete course in a profession.

ACNA Centre: the former Sycamore School, Hungerhill Road, St Ann's. Photo: Nottingham News Centre

They trained four people to do parts of the work required for one person as our primary role was to learn to fight and defend the country. I trained as a Wireless Operator for radars.

I was also stationed in Cornwall before being moved to north Devon. Crowds would come out to see these "blackies". There were places you could not go if you were black. People called you names in the street and you had to fight them.

CLASS DIFFERENCE
In the 1950s and 1960s, the Trade Unions fought for better facilities to improve industrial relations. It was not just our struggle alone but a general struggle of the working classes to bring about a more equitable distribution of facilities and opportunities, irrespective of class, status, race or country of origin. When I was a child in Jamaica, there was also prejudice there, the same as here.

However, in England, it was not just colour prejudice but prejudices based on class, ethnicity and religion. Catholics used to have lots of

problems but not as bad as how Muslims were treated. It was not until the Race Relations Act of 1965, did I see some changes in the way people were treated. People used to call you all sorts of names and the only thing you could do was to fight them. There seemed no point trying to take people who racially abused you to court - you had to just take it. Ironically, the first person to be convicted under the Race Relations Act of 1965 was a Caribbean person called Lee Fritas, a Trinidadian. He was convicted of abusing white society and sentenced to three months in prison.

In the early days of West Indian economic migration to Britain from the late 1940s onwards there were 'wars on words' between the different Caribbean groups: the Bajans (from Barbados), the Trinidadians, and those from St Kitts etc. There seemed to be a 'divide and rule' policy engineered by our colonial masters. We had to fight all of that. It was not just a fight against white society but also conflicts within different community groups.

THE ORIGINS OF THE AFRO-CARIBBEAN NATIONALS ARTISTIC CENTRE (ACNA)

The Afro-Caribbean Nationals Artistic Centre (ACNA) is a registered company; it is not a sole ownership. The name for ACNA came about through Louis Morgan. He wanted a centre to house 'coconut art', that is art produced using the shells of coconuts. He had the idea that we (Jamaicans) could set up a centre for artwork. That is how the name came about. The people who formed ACNA formed it for semi-political reasons and not for personal profit. The founders were myself, George Leigh, Charles Washington, Louis Morgan, Milton Crosdale and Junior Forbes among others. ACNA was set up to fight racism, industrial and racial inequality and all the bad things that affected our community.

ACNA was first housed in the old Bluecoat School off Mansfield Road, Nottingham. When it was about to be closed down, Nottingham City Council did not know what to do with it, so there was a suggestion that it should be set up as an International Community Centre so members of the community could rent rooms and carry out social activities.

Dorothy Wood, a community worker with Nottingham City Council, took an interest in securing better co-operation between blacks and whites; she asked Milton Crosdale to call a meeting to invite black organisations to find out how best to utilise the building. At this time, it was very difficult for non-white groups to get a room to rent, to carry out social activities (ironically, it was just as difficult to get a room to live in). At the time, the Black Power Movement was in vogue in America and it seemed to influence black culture and politics in England. At this time, we also had the Afro-Caribbean Union (the West Indian Union). Surprisingly, in the 1950s to the 1970s, there were many black organisations in Nottingham and across the UK.

At first, we rented premises on Derby Road in 1971/1972 and set up a Trust in 1973. We wanted to build our own community centre but when we calculated the cost, it was about £30,000. When we decided to get premises, we could not. We looked around for premises and were pleasantly surprised to discover a school building on Hungerhill Road

Pioneer for change: George Powe aged 78 at home in Mapperley, Nottingham. Photo: Nottingham News Centre

(the former Sycamore Primary School) closed down and dilapidated. The Bridge Trust passed the school over to Nottingham City Council as nobody wanted it and thus, the Council acted as caretaker as it was often vandalised.

Urban Aid, a European funding initiative, was created in 1975/1976 and became an important opportunity for inner city communities to apply for grants. I think the UK received about £90 million. ACNA was then floated as a limited company. We applied for and received a grant, which was supposed to be spent by 1977. However, we could not find suitable premises so we asked for a dispensation to allow us an extra year to spend the grant.

The rent for the old Sycamore Primary School building was set at £20,000 per year and we had no experience of running or managing a large organisation. The building was finally leased by the Council to ACNA for fifty years and we received a grant of £60,000. However, the grant was not enough to refurbish because of the extent of vandalism.

George Powe 1926 - 2013.

Photo: George Powe and Jill Westby Archives

Jill Westby, wife of the late George Powe.

Photo: Nottingham News Centre

The city council believed we could not fix the building (but we did) and only contributed 26% of the grant.

Regular members have recently thought about buying the building through the committee but this decision has never been followed through. I resigned from the ACNA Management Committee but was recently co-opted back in, in 2012.

So far, I have undertaken over forty years work supporting and helping to manage the ACNA Centre. ACNA now needs organisation and effective, financial leadership for the future.

George Powe died on the 9th September 2013.

©Norma Gregory
Written by Norma Gregory.

First published in Mojatu Magazine Issue M011 and courtesy of *Mojatu Magazine, Nottingham.*

A soldier's uniform from a Nottingham regiment.

Photo: Nottingham News Centre

CHAPTER 2

REFLECTIONS FROM DR DESMOND WILSON FORMER LORD MAYOR OF NOTTINGHAM (2002-2003 AND 2005-2006)

I was born on 29th December 1939, Hanover, Jamaica and I attended Middlesex Elementary School, now called Middlesex Primary School. I came to England, aged seventeen, in 1957 to join my aunt.

I spent a short time in my youth doing motor mechanics repairs but found this too dirty for me! After playing truant from the job, I went to the beach and was beginning to become a little tear away! When my mother found out, she said that she had spent too much energy and resources for me to waste my life away. Since she felt that my future wasn't looking too good, she decided to send me off to England to join her sister who was already settled in Nottingham, from 1956. Therefore, coming to England was not anything to do with me - it was my mother's decision and I never questioned her decisions. What I now know, is that I would not have achieved what I have achieved today without her guidance and wisdom.

JOURNEY TO 'SOMEWHERE'
I spent twenty-six days on a ship called *SS Montserrat*. It sailed to Genoa, Italy where we disembarked and travelled by train to Calais, France then crossed the English Channel to Folkestone by ferry. From then onwards, I took the train to London then another train to Nottingham. In those days, there were rail guards positioned at certain places within the station directing passengers arriving from the Caribbean.

After arriving at Nottingham Midland Station, I boarded a taxi and paid the fare of two shillings and six pence. I was told that somebody would meet me on my arrival at 49 Cranmer Street. By chance, I met this man called Ned walking down Cranmer Street and he directed me to number 49. I said to him:

Desmond Wilson.　　　　Photo: Bob Wallace PYKCHA

"Tell me some ting, how you get inna dis ya place?

"You got to go up and ring the doorbell!" he said with laughter.

My aunty greeted me at the door as I was two days late on arrival. She was surprised and very happy to see me.

EMPLOYMENT CHANCES
I came to Nottingham just before Christmas on the 12th December 1957 and it was very cold. As Christmas was approaching, my aunt said that I should sign on at the Youth Labour Exchange, on Castle Boulevard after Christmas. There was a Welfare Rights Worker designated for Jamaicans coming to Nottingham. She was a white lady. It wasn't until March or April of 1958, that I gained my first employment working in a flour factory.

My first job was to disassemble the machines and make sure they were ready for delivery. I worked near a Wheatsheaf Pub where I tasted English beer for the first time.

MY BUSINESS: *DES'S CAFÉ*

I used to run my own small business called *Des's Café*. Children sometimes played truant from school and used to come and talk to me about racist teachers and the difficulties they were experiencing in the education system. People came to the café from their work at Raleigh Cycles, John Players (cigarette factory) and other local factories and used to talk about the problems they were experiencing like immigration issues (for their families), employment, healthcare and housing.

There were quite a few organisations coming together and starting petitions to initiate change. *Des's Café* became a focal point for the community. With frequent petitions, a lot of pressure was put on the local authority and it was out of these petitions that provision for the black community grew. For example, ACNA officially opened in 1978, as premises were slowly being made available. Many people in the community used their skills to make the ANCA Centre purposeful.

The Indian, Pakistani and Afro-Caribbean Centres Project (JIPAC) was founded in 1983. This project helped people to access help and entitlements. Lyn Gilzean must also be credited for her duty and commitment to the community, particularly for her provision of the Luncheon Club for the elderly, which still runs today.

THE 1958 NOTTINGHAM RACE RIOTS

Many people think that the riots in 1958 started in Notting Hill, London but they first started one Saturday night on the 23rd of August 1958, in Nottingham.

A group of us had gone to a wedding party at 56 Lamartine Street. On our way back, we noticed that shops were still open at 5am on the Sunday morning. At this point, I did not realise that the riots had already started until I got home and turned on my rediffusion (radio). Apparently, the riots were triggered as a reaction to frequent attacks on West Indians and in particular, on Eddie Gayle who lived at 20 Cranmer Street. He was driving the prettiest car in Nottingham, which was an American Chevrolet. He was attacked with wooden planks and chains by racist youths from Nottingham, Liverpool and Manchester. He, and others, fought back and defended themselves, in fact the local newspaper, the *Nottingham Journal*, reported that the West Indian lads came together and responded very swiftly and bravely. The worst nights of rioting documented by Mike Philips and Trevor Phillips in their 1998 book, *Windrush: The Irresistible Rise of Multi-Racial Britain* gives a sense of the terror and violence witnessed at this bleak time in Nottingham's history.

Following these civil disturbances, the Jamaican Premier (Prime Minister), Norman Manley, visited Nottingham on Thursday 10th September 1958. He stated that Jamaicans needed to become more active in our communities and encouraged us to join trade unions. His opening words, given at a speech at Nottingham Council House, stated: *"West Indians are here to stay! They have got constitutional rights. They are British subjects with British passports!"*

Ironically, it was out of the Nottingham race riots that Mr Eric Irons was made a Magistrate and J.P., an appointment made by Nottingham City Council. His role was to deal with issues affecting the community. He was considered the 'Mr Fix It' and tried to do a good job with the little resources available to him. In addition, from the Nottingham riots of 1958, the Nottingham Carnival came out of this. Only then did funding for arts projects start to become more available and accessible to the Jamaican community.

REFLECTIONS ON MY ROLE AS A FORMER LORD MAYOR OF NOTTINGHAM

When I became the 672nd Lord Mayor of Nottingham in 2002 to 2003 and later, from 2005 to 2006, I was the first African Caribbean person to hold the post. When I took office, there were problems for me because there were about fifteen officers that served as Civics. They had never had the opportunity to serve an African Caribbean Civic before. I had to introduce many changes to staff practice, which some were not prepared to adapt to. Eventually, I had the support of the Chief

Cllr Des Wilson (right), Percy Dread (left), Eddie Neale and others at St Mary's Church unveil a plaque at the graveside of George Africanus in 2003 as Nottingham's first recorded African business entrepreneur. Photo: Courtesy of Ray Gale

George Africanus Green Plaque unveiled in 2003, next to the grave of George Africanus.

Photo: Nottingham News Centre

Executive and the Leader of the Nottingham City Council to ensure these changes were implemented.

Nottingham is a multicultural city. When requests came into the Civic Office from diverse communities, officers used to accept or ignore some requests. As mayor, I was not prepared to have this. I felt that there was not appropriate recognition across all sections of the community. When requests came in, I made sure myself, the deputy and sheriff met and responded to all requests. Some staff were eventually moved out of the Civic Office. It was not clear sailing as Mayor of Nottingham.

Many people think that being Lord Mayor of Nottingham was an achievement for me. It was not the pinnacle of all my achievements but more like icing on a cake.

I had been Chair of various committees previously and had worked on the Nottingham Regeneration Board, which helped to rebuild communities following the demise of the coal industry in Nottingham. I also

17

Councillor Desmond Wilson Lord Mayor of Nottingham 2002-2003 and again from 2005-2006.
Photo: Courtesy of Nottingham City Council

Des Wilson now lives between Nottingham and Jamaica.
Photo: Nottingham News Centre

helped develop training programmes through New College Nottingham and Nottingham City Council with Milton Crosdale and supported the launch of an educational scholarship programme with a school in Jamaica. Therefore, the role as Lord Mayor of Nottingham was in recognition of the work I had been doing in the city over many years.

ADVICE FOR MERLITA BRYAN, SHERIFF OF NOTTINGHAM (2011-2012), THE FIRST BLACK FEMALE (AND OF JAMAICAN HERITAGE) TO HOLD THE POST

As the first African Caribbean, Jamaican female to hold the post of Sheriff of Nottingham, she can play an active role in motivating women. Women need to take a leaf out of her pages as evidence clearly suggests we have the capacity to determine our own destiny through faith. Nottingham University has awarded me with an Honorary Doctorate of Laws, so all things are possible!

I now live in Jamaica and spend much of my time identifying educational needs and I am doing

my best to motivate people. I am looking forward to setting up a training project in Jamaica. It is an uphill task but I am prepared to brace the challenge that awaits me!

Leroy Wallace (1947-1991) housing pioneer and community activist. Photo: Courtesy of Tuntum Housing Association

18

CHAPTER 3

REFLECTIONS FROM MILTON CROSDALE OBE FORMER EXECUTIVE DIRECTOR NOTTINGHAM COUNCIL FOR RACIAL EQUALITY

I was born on the 11th January 1945 in Jamaica however, my adopted home is England, having moved to Nottingham in 1962. I have another foot in Sri Lanka, thus my feet are placed in three camps! I married a Sri Lankan and we wanted to stay in Nottingham.

I found out about England because my parents came here to settle in 1954. They came through a sense of adventure, of looking for a better life and economic self-sufficiency. My parents, like everybody else, thought they could pick up the mantle on the streets of England and then go back home to Jamaica.

I was eighteen when I left Jamaica. Incidentally, I am from a family of fourteen children. Some of my siblings died when they were young. I had other cousins here when I came to England so in terms of being supported, it was good. I had just completed high school in Jamaica and got my first job as a Laboratory Assistant at a sugar-making factory in Surge Island, St Thomas. My job was part of the team testing sugar content in rum. However, in England, I hoped to be a Clergyman by profession, as this was what I thought I should be and not a Chemist. I wanted to study Theology, so I could be attired in my robes of office – to dress up and perform! As it turned out, I am actually a Baptist and Baptists don't wear robes like Anglican and Catholic clergy.

I came to England by aeroplane, which cost about £85, the ship took longer but was cheaper priced at £75. I arrived in October 1962 and I felt it was cold and unfriendly. To make things worse, my family did not meet me at the airport so I had to take a train to the station in Nottingham (near what is now the Victoria Shopping Centre) by myself. I found my way to my parents' residence who were living in a large house called Wellington Villas off

Milton Crosdale, 2012.   Photo: Nottingham News Centre

Derby Road (Canning Circus). It was a three-storey building with open fires. This was strange for me to see because in Jamaica we didn't have open fires, as fires were mainly seen in open fields or in the kitchen. I remember how cold it was when I arrived in 1962, no warm clothes were prepared for me in advance so I appreciated the warmth generated by the coal fire.

'FIND A TRADE' INSTEAD OF MY PREFERRED CAREER

I enrolled at People's College then Clarendon College after which, I looked for jobs around Chemistry but that didn't work. I was told I needed better qualifications than I already had. I can't remember who but somebody had a strange thought that I needed to learn a trade. So I got a job with a firm of welders. I was the worst welder ever! I decided to leave this job and found employment at Raleigh Cycles located on Lenton Boulevard, Nottingham. My job description stated I was a Production Controller for Raleigh prams. We had to learn about every part of the pram and each part had a seven-figure serial number that had to be learnt from memory.

BICYCLES ARRIVING AT CARIBBEAN PORTS SHIPPED BACK TO RALEIGH, NOTTINGHAM

Raleigh, I believe, had to shut down because of the economic situation through competition from China who had a labour market that Nottingham just did not have. In China, they can produce at a more economical rate so it is very difficult to complete under these conditions. I left Raleigh Nottingham in 1968 staying less than a year.

Raleigh Bicycles, at first, did not employ black people. It was only when the Federation of the West Indies returned shiploads of bicycles back to England, saying the Caribbean Islands would not be buying any goods from Raleigh, that the firm, in all its stubbornness, began to change its employment policies so that jobs, at last, were available for the 2,000 applicants from the West Indian community who were eligible for work.

Shortly after the 1958 riots in St Ann's, the Premiers (Prime Ministers) of Jamaica and Barbados, Norman Manley and Grantley Adams, under the auspices of the then known West Indies Federation, had discussions with major employers and stated that if they were not going to employ Caribbean people, they would refrain from buying their bicycles and other products. It was only when these leaders spoke up and economic sanctions began to 'bite' British manufacturers, that companies changed their policies. That is why when I left Raleigh, I felt I always wanted to open doors for other people. In this respect, I am tempted to classify myself as a pioneer to some extent.

As a community, we are not successful economically. We are not committed to purchasing property and to use that property (albeit a house) to purchase another house thus, helping someone else by adopting the practice of buying collaboratively.

We are not thinking clearly about the impact of developing African Caribbean businesses. Look at the Radford area for instance - during the 1960s, both sides of Radford Road had Jamaican businesses. What happened to those shops? There were eight to ten pubs. Every night there were black people in those pubs. Now every pub or business on that road has been transformed. Jamaicans don't own them anymore.

If there are any failures on our part, it is the inability to grasp economic opportunities as and when they arise. We don't influence the economy of our city or country enough. We need to be providers of goods or services. We cannot always be consumers to influence the economy.

HOUSING ISSUES FOR JAMAICANS IN NOTTINGHAM IN THE 1950s AND 1960s

In the 1950s and 1960s, most Caribbean families did not secure private housing or a place suitable for their children to live or to study and as a result, many houses were multi-occupied with lots of families and children. The front room quite often became the bedroom; the living room became a place for playing dominoes and for eating. In reality, children had a difficult time because how does one educate children in cramped conditions and balance that with parents coming in late and tired from their jobs?

Think of yourself as a mother and wife in Nottingham in the 1950s or 1960s. You started work at 7 am, your husband is a Miner and is on shift work, working long hours and a fair distance from home. You, your husband and children are living in one room (you may have also left some children behind in Jamaica and they are on your mind). You are also financially supporting the family you've left back home by sending money each week. People treat you badly at work. You have to come home, often cold and damp, whilst attempting to separate work experiences from your family life. You are having to collect the children from a child minder who probably didn't pay much attention to them and is rude to you as well. In addition to this, your relationship with your husband is not working effectively and through these pressures, he is down the bookies and/or looking at other women on the

Len Garrison (1943-2003) educationalist and co-founder of the Black Cultural Archives in Brixton, London.
Photo: Courtesy of Black Star Publications

Association of Caribbean Families and Friends (ACFF) building directed by Len Garrison, now derelict.
Photo: Nottingham News Centre

street. While work was easy to get, if you asked for promotion or more money employers would laugh at you.

These scenarios were typical of many families who migrated to the city from the Caribbean and was part of the reason we, including the late Len Garrison, set up the African Caribbean Families and Friends (ACFF) Education and Study Centre on Beaconsfield Street, during the 1980s. Young people could go from their homes, study in a quiet place and meet others. However, those living further away from the city had a hard time accessing the ACFF Centre.

ON THE FOUNDERS OF THE NOTTINGHAM WEST INDIAN STUDENTS' ASSOCIATION (WISA)

Many on arrival in Nottingham, got involved in groups or formed their own organisations. As a 20-year-old student in 1965, I began liaising with a core group of other young intellects to form the bedrock of what was eventually known as the

Mr John Wray B.Ed, M Sc, J.P.
Courtesy of Pitman Browne Archives

21

Dr Ainsley Deer West Indian Students' Association.
Courtesy of Pitman Browne Archives

Victoria Morse former Mayor of the London Borough of Greenwich.
Courtesy Pitman Browne Archives

Nottingham West Indian Students' Association (WISA), along with Pitman Browne, George Leigh, Junior Forbes, Lee Arbouin, Vena Case, Lavonnie White, Ainsley Deer and others. I was its first President and Mr John Wray was Vice President. We created the WISA magazine with Ainsley Deer as its Editor. Mr Wray was one of the first students within our West Indian community to qualify as a teacher. Second to qualify within the Students' Association was Lee Arbouin, who during the 1980s, was famed for establishing Nottingham's first Saturday School Project at the UKAIDI Centre in Marple Square, Woodborough Road.

The first university place gained within our Association was accredited to (now) Dr Ainsley Deer, who studied at the University of Salford, Manchester. Ainsley is now a prominent business entrepreneur, lecturing at various business organisations in Jamaica. The first to qualify as a Doctor of Medicine was Neville Ballin, graduating in Medicine from both Salford and

Edinburgh universities. Neville now lectures across teaching hospitals the Caribbean region. I must not forget Victoria Case, now Victoria Morse, elected Mayor of the London Borough of Greenwich (1994/95). Finally, Mr Eric Irons OBE of Top Valley, Nottingham. He was deemed of great assistance to us. Each time we had an AGM, he was invited to preside as Chair. He became the first West Indian appointed as a Magistrate in 1962 and a Justice of the Peace (J.P.) in Nottingham and the UK serving for twenty nine years and became a campaigner of equality and equal rights for the community at large.

Pitman Browne later became WISA President in 1968. He took over the reins of leadership and found it necessary to incorporate Music and Drama within the overall mission statement. As a student of Classical Piano and Drama at Clarendon College, Pitman was poised to raise awareness of the arts by creating a drama group. The Music and Drama Committees were chaired by the late

Louis Morgan and he was mainly responsible for organising concerts and evening entertainment. Pitman Browne wrote the script for an in-house recording for the whole cast titled, *Musicana Symposium*. To date, he still has the LP available for listening pleasure.

WISA: TRYING TO MAKE A DIFFERENCE

As a community, we are good at starting things but not so good at finishing. As a people, we are blessed with good ideas and I have seen progress at the expense of many disappointments. When I moved to England in 1962, we tried our best to balance work and study. We wanted to work hard and persevere as we were not intending to stay here long. We were 'triers' in the sense that we really wanted to make a difference. I cannot think of a former member of WISA who hasn't gone on to make something beautiful of his or her life.

We formed links with students from Trent Polytechnic (now Nottingham Trent University) and met at the YMCA for regular meetings around issues to do with educational opportunities, better housing conditions, better police relations and unfair dismissals at work and so on. In all of this, we did not lose focus, given our main objective was centred around educating our community. We used to have debates amidst a flurry of eloquent and interesting speeches. WISA, though only spanning three and a half years, has accomplished much in the sense of nurturing a cohort of now qualified intellects, some of whom are already retired.

NOTTINGHAM'S RACE EQUALITY COUNCIL

How I got my role as Director of the Race Relations Council in Nottingham was rather unusual. Whilst returning from a conference at York University, a person I was sitting next to on the train, who also attended the conference said, "Milton we were impressed with you back there." I asked him what he meant. The conversation went on, "Would you be interested in working for the Race Relations Board?" I hadn't thought about it then said, "yes, why not."

WISA magazine cover.   Courtesy of Pitman Browne   **WISA magazine inside cover.**   Courtesy of Pitman Browne

The Race Relations Board was formed after the 1958 Race Relations Act and was established to investigate racial discrimination. The Commonwealth Citizens Commission was the body that investigated race relations.

The man on the train said, "Would you come and work for the Investigatory Body?" I had no idea that the man I was talking to was the Chief Executive, Tom Connolly. I said, "yes" and quickly gave him my details.

An application form and an interview date was subsequently sent through from Mr Connolly. Following this, I had an interview with the Regional Manager Mr Ted Ratnaraja as the Board had a Regional Office in Nottingham. They asked me if I would attend an interview in London. I did and one week later, I was appointed as Assistant Conciliation Officer at the Race Relations Board, covering the East Midlands.

My job was to investigate racial discrimination and prosecute potential offenders through the courts. So between three of us, we covered the areas of Northamptonshire, Kettering, Wellingborough, Leicester, Nottinghamshire, Derbyshire, Lincoln, Peterborough and Cambridgeshire during the 1970s. This has been my life. The offices were based on the fifth floor at Birbeck House, which sadly is no longer there. I stayed with the Racial Equality Board until 1976 when the new Board came under the Commission for Human Rights.

I later found employment with the Community Race Relations Council, off Mansfield Rd and headed the employment section where we carried out research. In 1980, I became Head of Community Race Relations in Derby. By this time, I had helped to set up the Afro Caribbean Artistic Centre (ACNA), which was officially opened, by (former) Councillor O.Watkinson O.B.E and His Excellency Mr Ernest Peart CD (from the Jamaica High Commission) on the 26th November 1978.

THE ORIGINAL ACNA COMMITTEE MEMBERS WERE:
Milton F. Crosdale, Chairman
Oswald George Powe, Secretary
Mr F.T Lewis, Treasurer
Miss Dorothy Smith
Mr Sullay Jalloh

Mr C George Leigh
Mr George Vaughn
Mr A Hylton
Mr Junior Berrenga Forbes
Parton - Miss Louise Bennett

I was also involved in setting up the Nottingham Indian and Pakistani Centre on Woodborough Rd, Nottingham, then connected with Derby in 1985 and became a Senior Race Relations Officer. Not much longer afterwards, I received an OBE for my work. Other officers I worked with were Imelda Reed who later became a Member of the European Parliament (MEP) and Alan Simpson, who later became MP for Nottingham. I was also a governor of New College Nottingham and a member of the Skills Council. I am currently Chair of Positive Action Training and Recruitment Agency (PATRA) at the Marcus Garvey Centre, Nottingham and still live a full life. I taught Race Relations at Clifton College and I have been an adviser for the BBC. I was also a Councillor for Derby City Council for almost eight years but I had no desire to wear a chain as a Mayor. I didn't want to join the chain gang.

PIONEERING SPIRIT OF BLACK TEACHERS IN NOTTINGHAM
The rise of the Nottingham West Indian Students' Association seemed to coincide with the gradually increasing spiral of new teachers who were graduating, one after another. No sooner than arriving as an ex-patriot from Jamaica in 1958, John Wray took to higher education where he qualified with a Teacher's Diploma from Clifton College in 1965 and then studied for a B.Ed. at Nottingham University, before going on to teach at Morley School.

After completing Teacher Training at Trent Polytechnic in 1973, Lee Arbouin later qualified with a Teaching Diploma leading to a B.Ed before being assigned to her first teaching post at the Alderman Derbyshire Comprehensive School, then onto Manning Comprehensive – the rest is history. As a firm believer in multiculturalism, Lee started the Steve Biko Saturday School as the Ukaidi Centre, St Ann's, Nottingham before going off to Sheffield to set up the Sheffield

United Multicultural Education Service (SUMES) attempting to approach education from a more African-centred point of view. However, in the mid1980s, she accepted an invitation from the Sheffield Educational Committee to serve in the capacity of Inspector of Schools (OFSTED), regionally then nationally.

Dr Ainsley Deer, after qualifying at Manchester University, returned to Nottingham to teach at Elliot Durham Comprehensive School to serve as a teacher in 1973. His saddest memory of Nottingham, ironically, is much to do with Huntingdon Primary School where he was demoted to a lower stream because the teachers convinced themselves he didn't have the capability to excel. He has certainly proven them wrong, now with a Master of Science (M.Sc) and a Master of Philosophy (M.Phil.).

Junior 'Berrenga' Forbes had eight months teaching experience as a Primary School Teacher before coming to the UK in 1961. On arrival, he was advised to pursue the 'O' Level and 'A' Level route before studying for a Bachelor's Degree and then for a Master's Degree at the University of Leicester. Subsequent to this, he became a guest Lecturer at the Trent Polytechnic in Nottingham during the 1980s.

I am so pleased that there are more African Caribbean school teachers, given that the overwhelming majority during the 1950s and 60s were white Europeans who knew so little of how to relate to the cultural needs of a child of African descent. Thankfully, Dr Cecile Wright, now a Professor of Sociology from our own community in Nottingham, has attempted to address this issue in her book entitled, *Black Youth Matters: Transitions from School to Success* (2010). I believe we currently need more research into childcare and childcare provision.

We need to look at these contexts. As a community, we could not walk into an estate agent to buy a house in the 1950s and 1960s. It was said that a twenty-five year mortgage could not be given to a black person as it was suggested that a black person's lifespan would be shorter and also, that the bank would not get its money back in repayments. As well as this, it was believed and

Professor Cecile Wright.　　　Photo: Bob Wallace PYKCHA

suggested that when a house was sold to a black person, the value of the other houses on the street would fall.

The Meadows and St Ann's areas in Nottingham, were considered by many as dumping grounds for new arrivals from the Caribbean. These houses were bad in the first place. Families were also pushed towards Clifton, Radford and Hyson Green. We didn't have the confidence or voting strength to lobby local government into targeting better residential areas.

REFLECTIONS ON THE NOTTINGHAM CARNIVAL

The Nottingham Carnival was set up through a combination of factors. When I became involved it was on its knees and about to be closed down. The carnival had reached a point where the money to host it had nearly ran out. There was also bad management. Then a housing association called Tuntum, established in 1988, stepped in to help, in 1999. The Nottingham Carnival Trust was then

Nottingham Carnival parade is an array of colour and vitality. Photo: Nottingham News Centre

formed. Richard Renwick, Chief Executive of Tuntum Housing now an MBE, had a large housing association to run as well as the carnival. As a skilled negotiator, he sought ways forward in order to secure financial support from local and national funding agencies. In effect, he also liaised with different community groups and centres, in order to oversee carnival legal planning and management requirements.

The majority of West Indians in Nottingham are of Jamaican heritage and not from Trinidad and Tobago where the Caribbean carnival originates from. I am not certain that Jamaicans understand what carnival is really about. There seems to be a lack of knowledge, which is now exchanged for passion and fun to channel engagement. The carnival should be like a flower blossoming; the planning is done all year, then flowering in the fullness of a massive parade on a glorious sunny day, thereby conveying its own story of a rich and colourful, historical past.

MY HOPES FOR THE FUTURE

Professionally, I feel little hope for myself now as I am sixty-nine years old and a diabetic with blood pressure. Even so, I would like to travel more, so I can learn more of the outside world. What of my three children? To date, they are still not classified as homeowners.

I would like to be better at my job as Lay Preacher at Pear Tree Road Baptist Church, Derby. I would like to be more focussed and ready to answer 'the call' especially if there is a need. Above all, let us hope that the Jamaican community will capture the vision of becoming more providers of goods and services within our present economy. Entrepreneurial business in the community is my greatest ambition. We need to take back what we gave away. We gave away the opportunity to run our own businesses or own the office block. We need to influence the market in a way as to become providers of goods and services not simply consumers.

Also, I would like to see more Jamaican accountants, lawyers, and head teachers in

Mr Bob Wallace, Chairman of the ACNA Centre, 2014.

Photo: Nottingham News Centre

Nottingham. We need more of our people in politics. Ronald McIntosh, Eunice Campbell, Tony Robinson, Hylton James, Des Wilson, Marcia Watson and Merlita Bryan, in their respective roles as Councillors, Sheriffs and Lord Mayors, couldn't have done more than what they have done as pioneers in local government. Thankfully, these pioneers have emerged as pace setters in their own right. I do not want to see Jamaicans taking the last seat at the back of the room in meetings, silent and not contributing. Instead, I want to see active participation in the dynamics of discussion and actions that create fruitful accomplishment. In terms of practical involvement in improving conditions, there is more to be done.

Lee Arbouin, author and a founder member of Nottingham's WISA.

Photo: Nottingham News Centre

Stephanie Marlow teaching the youth.   Photo: Nottingham News Centre

Grenadian Richard Renwick MBE, shares his thoughts on the Nottingham Carnival as its director since 1999.

Photo: Nottingham News Centre

CHAPTER 4

INKLINGS OF A GENIUS
AN INTERVIEW WITH PITMAN BROWNE
AUTHOR, POET AND PIANIST

Once a pianist, always a pianist. These are some of the buzz words articulated by Pitman Browne as we got to grips with the start of a long awaited interview.

Wearing his red African chamoise and sitting comfortably at the piano, Pitman was highly alert and ready to share his great talents, spanning fifty years, producing unique literature, music and video. He emphasised how these surroundings helped him relax and gain 'oneness' with self and the artistic environment, thereby making his otherwise seemingly nervous nature on the outside somewhat calm, confident and resilient on the inside.

Pitman has been a cornerstone of the African Caribbean community in Nottingham since his arrival from Kingston, Jamaica in September 1962, aged 17. However, over the last fifty years, he has been a huge contributor to the arts and literary movements in Nottingham and beyond. As a pioneer of community development through literature, music and film, the city of Nottingham and its residents, especially those hailing from St Ann's, have lots to be proud of primarily due to Pitman's efforts.

"All I was told about England at school was the existence of the BBC Symphony Orchestra conducted by Sir John Barbirolli enmeshed in all the glories of Parliament and Westminster Abbey!" said Pitman with his sardonic sense of humour.

He equates his, 'polka dotted experience' living in parts of St Catherine, Clarendon and Kingston, Jamaica with what he calls, 'a mixture of the good, the bad and the ugly'. "When I arrived in England, I felt cheated because of the weather and living conditions. So I enrolled at Clarendon College and studied Classical Piano (part-time), whilst working at Bairnswear knitwear factory in Basford. There was unemployment in the African Caribbean community but this was balanced out

Mr Pitman Browne, former President of the West Indian Students' Association now pianist, writer and performance poet.   Photo: Phullar Studios

with an equal chance of quickly finding another job – unlike now," states Pitman in his vocally poetic narrative, a mirror of his own unique writing style.

"1966 became a big turning point for me with the offer of a grant from Nottingham City Council to pursue full-time studies in Music, Drama, Language and Literature – an academic turning point, which also gave me a chance to meet students from across the city who were members of the Nottingham West Indian Students' Association.

During the first couple of years of arrival, I remember going round to people's houses for a fireside chat. Practically all the West Indian homes in St Ann's in the early sixties had an 'open door' policy and the

Pitman Brown aged 12 (right) with mother Mae Montomery and sister in Jamaica, 1957.   Courtesy of Pitman Browne

subject of discussion was mainly to do with the 1958 riots. Much of this is included in my book entitled, *Children Get Out of the Ghetto Mentality*, self-published in 2000. This book was written to question and explore youth subculture," says Pitman.

"There has been a breakdown of communication within our own West Indian culture. Broken relationships within the home followed by a prevalence of youth gang culture, the intake of banned substances, coupled with extreme forms of entertainment linked to the desire for quick money. Where are the massive seizures of drugs collated from drug dealers by the police? My book asks these questions," says Pitman with a tinge of anger and revulsion. "Some of my answers come from case studies and street talk. Within pages of my book, I also incorporate examples of improper policing on our streets."

At sixty-nine years old, Pitman has many strings to his bow. He is an established Author, having published five books and is a mentor and guide for emerging writers. As an exciting Writer and Performance Poet, he is poised as

an accomplished Interviewer and Videographer. To date, he has amassed over eighty videos on YouTube (see www.youtube.com/pitmanbrowne). As a finishing touch to his fascinating Curriculum Vitae, Pitman is also a composer of exceptionally unique, classical music. On top of all this, he is an accomplished Pianist, playing each week at the Upper Room Seventh Day Adventist Church and resident Organist at the Chasewood Baptist Church as well as serving the Wells Road Chapel, St Ann's in the capacity of Organist.

Pitman is a man not afraid to venture into subjects many with stable careers would probably stay well clear of. "My first book, *Inklings of a Black Christ*, published in 1998 by Kitabu-Pet Publications explores the premise that Jesus and the Apostles were African men. This book examines scholarly research findings on this hidden belief and attempts to turn around misconceptions to their true order," said Pitman with enigmatic passion.

Reflecting on his life and future, Pitman concludes the interview with reference to his autobiography titled, *What is My Mission* his last (but not final) book, shares his personal feelings and details aspects of his private life, "Women – a part of life I can't reach so I leave it alone!" says Pitman with a giggle. Lurking behind his enigmatic smile, he completes the interview by stating, "I am blessed nonetheless with two lovely sons: Theo aged twenty and Manley thirteen."

PITMAN BROWNE'S BOOKS:
Inklings of a Black Christ (1998)
Wishing Can Be Dangerous (1999)
Children Get Out of the Ghetto Mentality (2000)
Community Writing (2003)
What Is My Mission? (2005)

To order Pitman's books visit www.kitabu-pet.com

©Norma Gregory

Written by Norma Gregory.
First published in Mojatu Magazine Issue M011 and courtesy of *Mojatu Magazine,* Nottingham.

Pitman Browne (left) as President of WISA in 1968, Milton Crosdale (third left) presidents of WISA with friends.

Photo: courtesy of Pitman Browne

CHROMA Arts a charity that helped to support black writers in the 1980s. *Courtesy of Pitman Browne*

Chroma Arts publication.

Courtesy of Pitman Browne

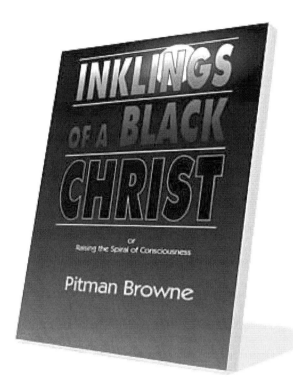

Pitman Browne's *Inklings of a Black Christ*, self-published in 1998.

Photo: courtesy of Pitman Browne

NOTTINGHAM WEST INDIAN STUDENTS ASSOCIATION
makings of a success story in each of us
First Successes

In 1968 Ainsley Deer was the first West Indian in Nottingham to be offered a place at University. Applause rang out as Milton Crosdale the President, made the announcement during the Students Association Sunday afternoon session.

Family friend, Tony Robinson, the then bus driver who years later became Sheriff of Nottingham, was so proud of the achievement of this 18-year-old youngster that he took him in his car all the way to Salford University (Manchester) for the inauguration.

Ainsley Deer

In 1965 John Wray was offered a place at the Teachers' Training College at Clifton — now re-named Nottingham Trent University. Subsequently, he became the first West Indian to graduate as Teacher in Nottingham.

In 1968, the year of his graduation he was offered his first post at Morley School in St Anns a post he held for some 12 years. Mr Wray incidentally, is now a resident in Ocho Rios, Jamaica.

John Wray

Excerpts from Pitman Browne's book, *What Is My Mission?*, self-published in 2005.

Courtesy of Pitman Browne

CHAPTER 5

REFLECTIONS FROM JUNIOR 'BERRENGA' FORBES
A FOUNDER MEMBER OF THE ACNA CENTRE

I was born in Spanish Town Jamaica, in 1945 but grew up in Vere, Clarendon, Jamaica where I attended Portland College Primary School: a combined infant, junior and secondary school. I heard about England by word of mouth as poster advertisements requesting labour work force appeared earlier, during the late 1940s and early 1950s. By the time it got to the 1960s, these adverts for workers had largely disappeared. People had relatives, who were already in the UK and this is what motivated many Jamaicans to come to England.

I left Jamaica when I was sixteen years old, on the 18th of March 1961. I had a job in Jamaica, working in an infant school where I had been teaching for about eight months. The school leaving age in Jamaica in the 1950s was fifteen, mirroring the education in England, its 'mother country' at that time. It was only in 1972, that the school leaving age in England was increased to sixteen.

In England, I went into higher education and studied for a Bachelor's Degree in Industrial Chemistry, Social Science and then for a Master's in Education at Leicester University. I felt I had a wide choice of career options. However, my family wanted me to stay in education so that was the reason I ended up studying Industrial Chemistry thus, rebelling against what my family wanted me to do. I eventually became a guest Lecturer at Trent Polytechnic, Nottingham teaching courses in Social Studies and Education.

I don't think many Jamaicans prepared sufficiently for coming to England. Most people simply came in search of a better life. My mother felt it was time for me to leave Jamaica when I did in 1961 and my father felt that if I stayed, I would perhaps drift into bad company. He said

Junior Berenga Forbes, ACNA Centre pioneer.

Courtesy of Junior Berenga Forbes

that I would be better off in England. Like many people in that period, there was the general belief that one would get better opportunities in England. On arrival in England, I stayed for a short period in London with one of my uncles. I later moved to Nottingham and was accepted to study at People's College. Even though I did some teaching in Jamaica, I had to do my O-Levels all over again. This was the experience of many West Indian people who came to England with qualifications from overseas. I also needed to pay for the cost of travel, books and examinations.

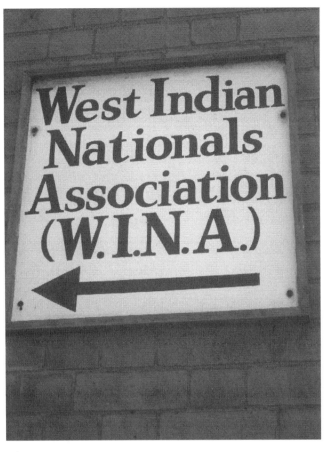

W.I.N.A. building. Photo: Nottingham News Centre

PERSPECTIVES ON THE ORIGINS OF THE AFRO-CARIBBEAN NATIONALS ARTISTIC CENTRE (ACNA)

The Afro-Caribbcan Nationals Artistic (ACNA) Centre was primarily started through a coalition of local organisations. However, the people in the coalition were mainly from an organisation called the Black People's Freedom Movement (BPFM). The BPFM were the ones who really started ACNA. George Powe was the secretary of the BPFM. I was the Chairperson and Henry Lewis (now living in Florida) was the Treasurer. There were twelve people on the committee: eleven of them were members of the BPFM. There was one person from the West Indian National Association (WINA) and that was Mr George Leigh, now deceased.

We persuaded members of the BPFM to step down so that we could have more of the other group (WINA) involved. We were trying to make a confederation so that the organisation would not be seen as dominated by what was seen as a radical group of young people (the BPFM). Therefore, members of the BPFM resigned in order for elections

to take place so that the committee vacancies could be filled by people from WINA.

There was also another group called the West Indian Students' Association. The three groups shared a building at 126a Derby Road, Nottingham from about 1971 to 1978. It was the office before ACNA office moved on the 13th September 1978 into what was the Sycamore Primary school on Hungerhill Rd, St Ann's. It was from its original base at Derby Road that the planning and development of ACNA took place from 1972 to 1977.

FUNDING GRANTED

Funding for ACNA Centre came under Section 11 Grant Aid Phase 14, which gave grants to community projects. The centre was supposed to be self-funded and purchased through the Committee. We wanted the money gained from the bar at ACNA to be a major funding resource, to bring in income to cover costs. We had a building fund. Through membership contributions, we were supposed to be saving to purchase our own building. I do not know what

George Leigh's funeral.

Photo: Nottingham News Centre with kind permission from Kate Hayward became of that. Unfortunately, the vision for the centre has changed.

ACNA Centre officially opened in 1978 with the aim to develop a community facility for people from the Caribbean because at that time, there was, what seemed to be, a small Afro-Caribbean community in Nottingham. It was to provide a place where people could eat and enjoy the benefits of a social club and a venue to develop the arts. We aimed to provide opportunities for local talent to be developed and 'exposed' as well as facilitating guest artists and community entertainment, not forgetting educational seminars.

I felt that the BPFM had made a mistake in that it wanted unity at any cost. Some members were only interested in the social side of the club. Dominoes and cricket became the focus, especially in terms of committee member voting. Committee members voted for others who were interested in dominoes and cricket as opposed to core issues. This caused disputes in terms of the use of the building as well as the philosophy and ethics of the centre. We found that one or two of the neighbours initially used to complain about the noise levels. However, that did not last very long. We had very good PR representatives who would visit and talk with neighbours and local businesses. We invited them to functions. One complaint we had was the slamming of car doors at 2am in the morning when the crowds from a dance or party were milling about.

For the African Caribbean community the response for the ACNA Centre was tremendous.

Junior Berenga Forbes, new home in Gambia.

Courtesy of Junior Berenga Forbes

Tony Brown, former manager of the ACNA Centre. Photo: courtesy of the ACNA Centre

Barbecue Jamaican style. Photo: Nottingham News Centre

George Leigh, manager, assesses the fire damage at the ACNA Centre, January 1987. Courtesy of the Nottingham Evening Post

The first month of the centre being opened, Kenny and I took time off from our paid employment to work voluntarily. He took two weeks off and I took one month off. We managed the centre ourselves thereby demonstrating that in the first month we could successfully run the centre. It was as if the African Caribbean community had been 'starved' of something they felt was their own. It was tremendous.

We had people begging us if they could assist in the bar, or even just collecting glasses and bottles. People just wanted to be involved. We then felt we were able to appoint a Centre Manager called Tony Brown. He was appointed as Club Manager. In 1986, I felt I could no longer be part of the management of ACNA. I left Nottingham and worked in several parts of the UK before moving to Gambia in 2008.

Ronald McIntosh (1925-2012), Sheriff of Nottingham, 1994-1995. Photo: Courtesy of Stephen McLaughlin

Randolph Richardson of St Kitts, a pioneer of the Nottingham Carnival in the 1970s along with James 'Woody' Heyliger of St Kitts organiser of the first Nottingham Caribbean Carnival in 1958. Photo: Nottingham News Centre

CHAPTER 6

REFLECTIONS FROM ARNOLD 'KWAME' WRIGHT
CULTURAL ACTIVIST

THE NOTTINGHAM CARNIVAL

Before the Nottingham Carnival, as we now know it, local folks used to organise summer festivals in the Arboretum Park during the early 1970s. There was music and dance with bands such as the Black Diamonds, Myra Mead with Charles Washington acting as MC. This was when the whole community would come out and enjoy the festivities. The Nottingham Carnival then came out of this. The carnival used to be the weekend before the Notting Hill Carnival in London.

In the early days, the Nottingham Carnival was funded by Chroma Arts, through the help of Randolph Richardson. There were attempts to move away from the City Council to source funding streams elsewhere since, on a number of occasions, there have been financial cutbacks. This made carnival financially unsustainable - much to the dismay of the general public.

In terms of an appropriate venue, organisers decided that the Forest Recreation Ground site on Gregory Boulevard, would be good to allow a carnival processional route on the streets of Radford with stalls so that people could come out of their homes and sell food such as fry fish just like in the Caribbean. The great advantage of a huge park space is the ability to invite neighbouring cities like Leicester and Derby to join us, to make the carnival bigger.

Also on the agenda for consideration was the Victoria Embankment site near the Meadows area and not far from Trent Bridge. This was the original site the Nottingham Carnival took place for about two or three years during the late 80s and early 90s. After this, I did not have much involvement. There was then a move to the Forest Recreation Ground with a selection of administrators trying to manage the carnival and all its challenges. The

Arnold Wright, Community Activist and former ACNA Treasurer.
Photo: Nottingham News Centre

current management and custodian is Tuntum Housing Association through Richard Renwick, Chief Executive of Tuntum Housing and Chair of the Nottingham Carnival Trust.

STEEL FENCING

For me, the metal security ring fencing is more or a big, psychological problem. At the moment, I don't go to the current carnival because I refused to be imprisoned. The ring fencing reminds me of a slave plantation - I do not see why we need a ring fence. Security could be done in a way where we don't see it. Goose Fair, held on the Forest Recreation site, is secured differently and with less of an eyesore.

Charles Washington, 2013. Photo: Nottingham News Centre

Delroy Brown, former Nottingham Carnival management member with Leslie Davis, around 1993-1997.

Photo: Nottingham News Centre

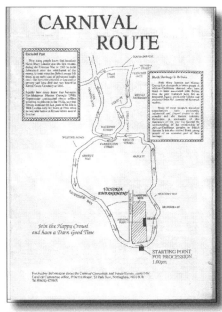

Carnival route plan, 1991.

Courtesy of William Stewart.

Cover of Nottingham Carnival brochure, 1991.

Courtesy of William Stewart.

Carnival programme, 1991.

Courtesy of William Stewart.

Nottinghamshire Police Commissioner, Paddy Tipping (centre) with Catherine Ross (left), formally open the Nottingham Carnival, 2014.   Photo: Nottingham News Centre

Nottingham Carnival, 2014.   Photo: Nottingham News Centre

Arnold Kwame Wright lectures on African history, Jamaica Independence Day 2012.   Photo: Nottingham News Centre

UK Trini and Friends, Nottingham Carnival 2014.   Photo: Nottingham News Centre

Arnold Wright educating a group of pupils visiting the ACNA Centre, 2011. Photo: Nottingham News Centre

Nottingham vendor. Photo: Nottingham News Centre

Nottingham Carnival crowds enjoy the music. Photo: Nottingham News Centre

Trinidadian born William Stewart, community activist and Nottingham Carnival management in the early 1990s. Photo: Nottingham News Centre

Arnold Wright proud to wear his African attire.

Photo: Nottingham News Centre

CHAPTER 7

REFLECTIONS FROM VERNON GREGORY 'KING' FORMER COAL MINER

My name is Vernon Gregory. 'King' is my nickname from earliest memories, back in Jamaica. Up until now, family and friends still address me as 'King'. I was born in Riversdale, St Catherine in 1931. Our family consisted of five male siblings: Darlton, George, Alteman, Joe, myself and my sister. I went to Mount Hermon School in Riversdale, in the district of Hampshire, then came to England when I was twenty-five years old as my brother, Alteman invited me to join him here. Alteman came to England in 1954 and I followed on the 14th May 1956.

I don't remember seeing any posters or adverts in Jamaica promoting migration to England. I came through my brother's invitation, and he chose to settle in Nottingham, which is why I came to Nottingham. Sadly, my brother has since died.

In Jamaica, I worked as a farm hand on a sugar cane plantation in Spanish Town for a man called 'Lindo'. Before I left Jamaica, people listened to Reggae music, Jazz as well as Rhythm and Blues. Artistes would come from America, like Louis Jordan (1908-1975) who was very popular then. In Jamaica, we used to go to the theatre to listen to music groups, one of which was young Bob Marley and the Wailers.

CAREER INTENTIONS

When I came to England, I hoped to find a better job because there were not many jobs in Jamaica. I came here with the intention of doing *any* work and staying for only ten years but after more than sixty years, I am still here! One of the reasons I remained here was because of family. In 1957, I sent for my girlfriend, 'Blanche'. She was of Indian decent. We got married in 1962 and had five children (Blanche died in 1999, aged 72) I decided not to go back to Jamaica because of my family's upheaval and the

Vernon 'King' Gregory, former Gedling Colliery Coal Miner.
Photo: Nottingham News Centre

cost to relocate again. Also, wages were very low in England and I could not even find the money to return. I have only returned to Jamaica once, in 1976 on the occasion of and subsequent death of my mother, Ettelle Gregory. She was married to my father called Josiah Gregory. I have no intention of ever returning permanently to Jamaica to live, after being in England for so long.

I travelled to England on a ship called, *Captain Verdic.* it was an Italian ship. The ship left from Kingston, Jamaica. My ticket cost £75, which was a lot of money in those days. I saved and paid for my own ticket. I brought one suitcase and a little holdall. We were on the ship for fourteen days. The sea was quite rough but some parts were calm. I remember the boat rocked a lot! There were not all Jamaicans on board. As we stopped at different countries to collect passengers, there was an influx of folks of different nationalities. I made some friends on the boat, some of whom were Jamaicans. We did not know where we were going really, so were had to be friendly!

We sailed from Jamaica to Italy and then on to England, where we docked at Southampton. We then took a ferry to London after which we reported to the Immigration Office. They checked us out. From there, I made my way to my brother's accommodation. He had given me instructions for travelling to Nottingham. I followed his instructions and took a train from Victoria Station to Midland (Nottingham) station, then took a taxi to my brother's address. He could not meet me because he was at work and could not afford and was not allowed to take the day off to meet me. When I arrived at the house, somebody was there to let me in. My brother and I shared a room. I remained with him for about one year before finding my own accommodation.

FINDING EMPLOYMENT
Before I came to England, I thought England was a nice place for promoting prosperity where one could work for a lot of money. However, when I came and saw conditions of abject poverty and low pay, plus the shock and dismay on the faces of other Jamaicans like myself, I came to the conclusion that there was no turning back. This is Britain!

In 1956, people had to go to the Labour Exchange to sign on for employment. The Labour Exchange knew where all the job vacancies were and you were sent to various places. Also in those days, you did not wait for the Labour Exchange alone to find work, but could ask other people and approach different factories for yourself. One of my first paid jobs in was car spray-painting for Vauxhall Car Company, in Castle Boulevard, where I was paid seven pounds, eleven shillings per week, in 1956. I found that saving money was difficult on a low wage, so I worked there for six months. I did not really like the job because the money was not good so I changed jobs quite often. I came to

England with the intention of getting a well-paid job. I found a job at the Coal Board, working on the ground (surface). Again, the pay was not very good so I left and went to work at James Hole and Company Brewery, on Albert Street in Newark-on-Trent, Nottinghamshire for two and a half years. After this, I went back to the Coal Board, but this time worked down in the mines at Gedling Colliery until 1979.

WORKING AT GEDLING COLLIERY
Working at Gedling Colliery was a very dangerous job. You had to look after yourself when you were several feet down below. I worked in the pit for twenty-seven years and I was there during the turbulence and upheaval of strikes amongst the miners from around 1972 to 1985. We had to go on the picket lines to protest and try stopping others crossing the picket lines. Some miners ignored the strike and carried on working regardless; as such, they said they could not afford to strike because of 'family commitments' (large families).

The last strike in 1984 was a bad one. Many pickets came down from Yorkshire and used to threaten miners, trying to scare them into strike action. There was a chap who said to me that if I went down the pit, he knew where I lived and would do something to me or my family. During the strike, I was off for six weeks, with no money, so I had to go back to the Labour Exchange for money to live on. I was made redundant from the Coal Board in 1986. Since then, I have not worked. I was aged fifty-five at the time and jobs were difficult to get back then.

REFLECTIONS OF THE NOTTINGHAM RACE RIOTS, 1958
The Nottingham race riots were in St Ann's, in August 1958. I did not get involved in it because I was living in Lenton. It didn't last long because of police intervention. When Jamaicans came in the 1950s, some lads called 'Teddy Boys' attacked West Indians, mainly Jamaican men. They thought that they could beat up black people as they liked. They did not know that black people would fight back and defend themselves. Black people were not an easy walkover.

CHAPTER 8

REFLECTIONS FROM CALVIN WALLACE 'WALLY' FORMER COAL MINER

My name is Wally and I was born in the Parish of St Ann's, Jamaica in 1930. I was 29 years old when I came to England in November 1959. Back in Jamaica, I went to Enion Town Boys' School, in the Parish of Clarendon. I have never been to college to pursue any level of formal education. However, in Jamaica, I worked in farming, on a plantation, which was my family's land and in reality, a major contribution to my learning and preparation for my life's journey.

ADVERTISEMENT ABOUT ENGLAND IN JAMAICA

I found out about coming to England through an advert. 'If you want a better life come to England,' the poster said. Before I left Jamaica, I went to work in America for a few months to save some money. After saving up, I told my mother I was leaving Jamaica with my brother to seek a better life in England. Most people knew somebody who had already gone to England and then got in touch with them. I tried to get an invitation in order to seek work.

I didn't know what the climate was going to be like but I was told that it was not warm here. My suitcase was packed with my khaki, shirts and shoes. As for our mother, she gave me and my brother her blessing and wished us well.

We came on the ship *Escalla* and travelled for twenty-one days. Our tickets cost £75 each. I ate, slept, went on deck and had a laugh. The ship stopped first in Dominica Republic before arriving at Southampton, England. The journey was enjoyable but when we arrived, we did not realise how cold it was. I had about £30 in my pocket, which came in handy. These were the pre-decimal days when £30 was a lot of money. I had no job arranged in England.

Calvin Wallace aged 29 in Nottingham, 1959.

Photo: Courtesy of Calvin Wallace

HIGH EXPECTATIONS

England was presented in Jamaica as our 'mother country'. There were adverts showing how people we getting on well so much so, we were misled into thinking that prosperity was at our finger-tips purely by the click of our fingers. Many Jamaicans thought that if you were white, you were rich. When we came and saw the extent of poverty and overcrowding and lack of sanitation, it breathed a new sense of culture shock. However, there was a Jamaican community already here in Nottingham and I also found out that there were Jamaicans living in Sheffield, Birmingham, London and other cities.

Wally and Jean Wallace (left) in Nottingham with family, 1982.
Photo: courtesy of Calvin Wallace

Pensive, Wally Wallace.
Photo: Nottingham News Centre

ARRIVING IN NOTTINGHAM, 1959

From Southampton, I took the train to London then changed for another train to Nottingham. From before leaving Jamaica, we were advised to be on the alert, be careful and act as if we knew what we were doing. A minister in a church had a brother-in-law who was living at Albert Grove, Nottingham and he put me in touch with someone who would receive us.

My brother and I arrived at night and all we could see were chimneys. "What a lot of factories!" I thought The taxi driver said these were not factories, but people's houses. It was very cold, with snow. If you hung your clothes outside on the line, they would be black with soot and smoke from the chimneys and coal burning. We had paraffin heaters in the room.

I used to go to a Baptist church in Lenton, Nottingham. Some of the congregation came and talked to me and others turned their faces in the opposite direction. This to me was unthinkable. I didn't believe some white people could be so rude and unfriendly. The way England was portrayed in Jamaica, we were taught to believe that everyone would be civil. However, when we arrived, it was totally different. Some people were alright while others were really horrible to you, calling you, "black bast_rd," and 'black this' or 'black that'.

FINDING EMPLOYMENT

My first job was doing mouldings at the Beeston Boiler Company, off Queens Road, Nottingham in 1961 then I left in 1976 to work at Raleigh Bicycle Factory. After that, I went to work at the pit, Gedling Colliery, from 1976 until 1987. During the 1980s period of the miners' strike, Gedling Colliery was not on strike. Arthur Scargill sent many men from Yorkshire with police escorts. Some worked through the strike and were called, "scabs" and all sorts of bad names. All the men who did not work and were on strike lost their homes. Nevertheless, the man who took them out on strike still had his home well

Gedling Colliery a coal mine from 1898-1991 now derelict and to become a 240 acre country park in 2015. 130 people lost their lives at the pit during the 93 years it was open.

Photo: Nottingham News Centre

secured. He was getting money both ways: from the workers and from the government. When the strike was finished, you no longer had people calling you a scab, so everyone was alright. However, you still had the 'scar' because other miners knew who came from Nottingham and people would say, "You see him, he is one of them!" I was made redundant from Gedling Colliery in 1987.

MY REFLECTIONS ON THE NOTTINGHAM RACE RIOTS, 1958

The Nottingham race riots took place in St Ann's in 1958. As a West Indian, you could not walk on your own in certain places or at certain times. You had to walk in threes or fours. The 'Teddy Boys' went around with bicycle chains. When they saw three of four Jamaicans together, they would not attack us as we were in a group. A lot of them got 'cut up' in St Ann's during the riots.

One thing I should have done since living in England was to learn to drive. I didn't like driving.

There are many things you gain from this country without realising it.

I married Jean McKenzie on the 28th February 1961 and I have only been back to Jamaica three times. I went to my mother's funeral and have not been back since.

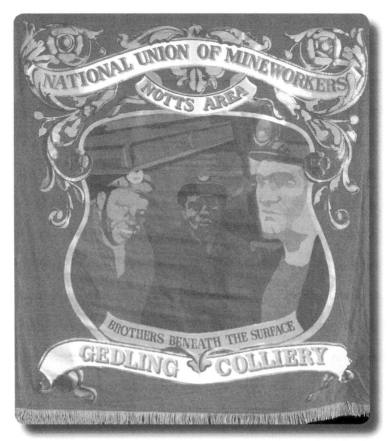

Gedling Union banner (front). Gedling Colliery was known as 'the pit of nations' due to the number of men from different nationalities working as miners in the pit. Image: Courtesy www.miningheritage.co.uk

Gedling Union banner (reverse). Image: courtesy of www.miningheritage.co.uk

CHAPTER 9

REFLECTIONS FROM OSCAR ROBINSON
FORMER RAILWAY WORKER

My name is Oscar Robinson and I was born on the 19th January in 1937. I am 77 years old now and I was twenty-four years old when I came to England on 12 May 1961. I was born in St Catherine, Jamaica and attended Mount Herman School.

My mother and father never lived together. My mother's name was Clarista Endison and my father was called Douglas Robinson, who came from St Elizabeth, Jamaica. He was a nice man. Sadly, my father was killed in Kingston. A mad man hit him in the head and his brains scattered on the ground and his leg was broken. This was in 1957 when I was twenty years old.

I did not have a permanent job in Jamaica so I did everything and anything to get by. I used to raise and breed nine hogs. I had the opportunity to come to England before 1961. My uncle wanted me to come to England in 1955 and again in 1956. I told him I was not coming to a cold country because I was better off living with my girlfriend in Jamaica. When I eventually decided to come, I left her and four children behind. I felt bad but thought I was coming to a place where I could make life easier by providing for them financially, by sending money home.

WHY DID I COME TO ENGLAND?

I did not cultivate any rosy visions about 'mother country' and the rest of it. All I wanted was a job so I could save money and head back home. Before leaving Jamaica, I worked in joinery and the mason trade. I wanted to be a motor mechanic but my father would not let me, as it would cost a lot of money to train for this career. Whilst I worked at Bybrook Sugar Estate, a foreman there encouraged me to learn joinery with him. With this, I made my decision to migrate to England, as life was getting much harder in Jamaica. There was not a

Oscar Robinson aged 24 in 1961. Oscar's first passport photo to travel to England.   Courtesy of Oscar Robinson.

lot of money around, no jobs and no work. I made my mind up then set about financing my travel arrangements.

There were no adverts or posters around advertising jobs in England. I came to England by invitation as my uncle was already here. My mother and uncle helped me save the money to pay for the flight ticket of £85. However, I heard about the good life people were having on the boat, so I got a refund for the aeroplane ticket and travelled to England on a boat called, *TVS Escavia*.

We sailed to Southampton, England. It was a non-stop journey, lasting twelve and a half days. Most boats stopped at other countries but this one did not, it went straight through. There were many people from other countries and many Jamaicans. I

49

Oscar Robinson living at 1 Mansfield Road, 1962.
Courtesy of Oscar Robinson

Dedicated railway employee Oscar Robinson
Photo: Nottingham News Centre

talked to lots of people on the boat who were going to different cities in England. When I came off the boat, I remember thinking all the buildings with chimneys were factories (*laughter*) but they were houses. I thought getting a job would be easy because of all the factories but they were houses!

I packed clothes in my suitcase and planned to stay in England for five years as most people did and then to fly back home. However, I have been here for over fifty years now (*laughter*). There was no special job in mind. Basically, I was unskilled except for masonry and joinery and was prepared to try my hand at anything at the time.

FINDING A PLACE TO LIVE

My first accommodation was an attic room my uncle found for me. I lived in Peel Street and rented one room. Another West Indian was living in a neighbouring room. He was from Barbados and was working on the railway. He encouraged me to apply for a job on the railway. Previously, I had applied

for a job at the pits and on the buses after which I decided to work on the railways, a decision I have never regretted. My uncle and aunt helped me settle in. They showed me how to do laundry and cook my own dinner. I then went to live at Heskey Street. At first, I thought the locals were 'stuffy nosed' but it was even worse for Jamaicans who came earlier in the 1940s and 1950s.

FRIENDSHIPS

I met my friend, Donald Gregory from Saint Catherine, Jamaica in the street. I was walking near Mansfield Road, Nottingham and my old friend from back home walked up to me and called out "Mass (Mister) Oscar". I was excited to see him, in fact I had no idea he was planning to come to England.

I helped him find work at Beeston Boilers, Queens Road and we remained good friends ever since. *(Donald Gregory died in March 2011)*. I met my first wife, Vina, at 16 Peel Street. She used to come to see her sister who was living down stairs.

Oscar Robinson, a Train Guard.

Photo: courtesy of Oscar Robinson

During late evenings, I use to go to the Calypso Club on Byard Lane, a social club set up by the Jamaican, Nottinghamshire cricketer, Mr Carlton Forbes. It was nice. I knew Carlton quite well, but he is now deceased. Because I had my own car, I could drive to see different places. I used to go to Sheffield, Mansfield, Derby and London. I helped many people especially when it came to transporting Jamaicans to the airport or bringing them back home.

WORKING FOR MIDLAND RAILWAYS
I was based in Stapleford when I first worked with the railway and I did shift work. I worked on the train engines but eventually applied for a job as a Train Guard. When I got this job, I was able to hire purchase a car for myself. At the time in the 1960s, you could count on your hand the number of African Caribbeans who had cars. I bought a Ford Anglia for £500. It was two years old. That car, brand new in those days, cost £700.

I was employed as a Freight Guard, a Train Guard, Conductor and then promoted to Senior Conductor. At one point, I was tempted to leave the job because of low wages but I stuck at it through perseverance. I was paid seven pounds, thirteen and six a week. I started out as a Freight Guard in 1961 but later transferred from Stapleford to Nottingham to work on the passenger trains.

I had a rough time working with passengers on the trains. I had people spit in my face; others pushing me about and some saying, "You should not be doing this job!" Some were prejudiced. To see a black man walking down the train aisle asking for, "tickets please," they did not like it. I 'lived' at work as I often worked seven days a week for twelve hours a day. But I was 'in charge' as I could not walk away from my duties and leave the train without another staff taking over. I got paid plenty of overtime and learned to save my money over the years. Now I am retired,

Goose Fair, Nottingham. Photo: Nottingham News Centre

I still get a free train pass for my (late) wife and myself. I don't go anywhere with it now though.

I am glad I did not leave the railways because I have a good pension. I put a lot of money into my pension so when I retired, I left work smiling! I requested redundancy in 1998 because I needed to take care of my wife who was ill with cancer. At first, they told me yes but then they changed their minds and said no because I was doing a good job for them. I had to go to my trade union for support

and advice before they decided to let me go. I was sixty-three and a half when I retired.

WHAT HAVE I LEARNT?

I have learnt many things living for over fifty years in England. England is like coming to college really. You still have many people who come and don't improve their knowledge or life chances. I think I have done well. However, one thing I don't like is loneliness now I am older. This is not a good thing but I am happy.

Rose Thompson, Director of BME Cancer Communities and an advocate for cancer awareness.

Photo: Courtesy of BME Cancer Communities

Lyn Gilzean, for many decades organised the West Indian pensioners' lunch club.

Photo: Courtesy of the ACNA Centre

CHAPTER 10

REFLECTIONS FROM WESTERN VACCIANNA
FORMER CHURCH MINISTER

I was born on the 29th of January 1933 but my birth was not registered until 15th February 1933 in the Westmoreland district of Jamaica. I am one of ten siblings: four sisters and six brothers. At sixteen, I worked in a cigar factory that used to supply cigars to the Chinese shops in Jamaica. At home we raised chickens, grew red peas and tobacco on six and three-quarter acres of my father's land to earn and to save money. It was hard work. I left Jamaica aged twenty-three.

BETTER LIFE AHEAD

I thought England was a land of opportunity as I had heard lots of wonderful things from a friend who was living there. At that time, I had a brother living

Western Vaccianna, 1956.   Courtesy of Western Vaccianna

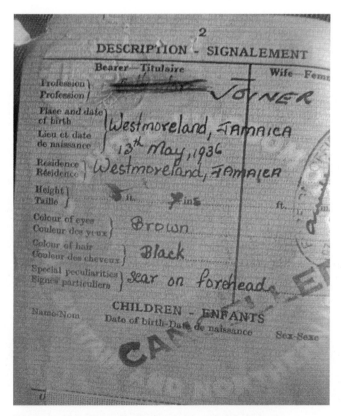

Western Vaccianna's first passport with stamps.

Courtesy of Western Vaccianna

in Sheffield who, in fact, arrived a year before I did. It was largely through correspondence with a friend in Nottingham that I decided to take the plunge and move to the UK.

At long last, I arrived on the 15th September 1956 after leaving Jamaica on the 6th August. I packed my suitcase and carried a windbreaker jacket in preparation for the cold. The boat on which I travelled was called *Santa Maria* and the ticket cost £75. There were many different people aboard and I remember it had seventy-five lifeboats and a swimming pool but I was not eager to use the pool, I just wanted to arrive safely in England. I brought twelve pounds since I was advised I needed to travel with at least two pounds. I arrived at Midland Station and took a taxi to 2 Addison Street, Nottingham and noticed every house seemed to have a chimney. There were

Western Vaccianna wedding day with first wife, 1957.   Photo: Courtesy of Western Vaccianna

four people living in my room: one in each corner. I found another room to rent soon after.

I had a friend called Roderick who was taken out of his bed at night by police and taken to join the Army. They banged the door: you know when it is a police officer because they knock viciously. They took away my friend even though his wife was expecting a baby. I was working at the railway so they did not bother me.

RELATIONSHIPS

I married my girlfriend who I left back in Jamaica in 1956. She joined me a year later and we got married in 1957. We had seven children but she later died. I married my second wife, Jane Anderson ('Miss Joseph') on the 1st December 1991. Jane passed away on the 12th February 2014.

THE CHANCE OF EMPLOYMENT

The Labour Exchange offered two pounds to each foreigner (when they first arrived) to buy food, clothing and so on. However, many Jamaicans never wanted this as it felt like they were living, as Jamaicans put it, 'in the poor house,' like back home. It did not matter how hard things were, we did not like accepting these handouts as somehow, we would manage. Sometimes friends would help until payday or until you received a payout through a 'pardoner' a community saving scheme for people who did not have bank accounts.

I received my wages every two weeks. I often worked six days a week on the building sites because there were not many people working on build sites back then. People could change jobs easily in the late 1950s and early 1960s because houses and building were being built following World War II. I enquired where factories were to find work as my friends had found jobs on the railways so I said I might as well try the railway to get a job.

In 1956, I started a job at Netherfield train station, which lasted for six months. Most people worked shifts. In my first job, I only earned six pounds and thirteen shillings a week. My boss was Mr Livic. No black men were allowed to drive trains, that was the saying in those days. Black people were not allowed to pass their train-driving test. We were not wanted

Sherwood Rooms, a hot spot for dancing in the 1950s and 1960s, now the Ocean Nightclub. Photo: Nottingham News Centre

Ocean Nightclub, formerly the Astoria Ballroom and the Sherwood Rooms. Photo: Nottingham News Centre

and considered not educated enough to drive trains. I left that job to get better pay and found a job at Radcliffe Power Station working with the sprinklers where I got double the wages: twelve pounds. Each tower carried about eleven thousand little sprinklers. My job was to fix them on. One day, I cut my hand very badly and was off work so I had to leave after nine months because of this accident.

My next employment was building and construction work: helping to build bridges, in fact, I was part of a team who were sub-contracted to do certain jobs. I passed my driving test in 1970 and bought a new twelve-seater van. I used it to take people to and from work as well as moving them around, in and out of Nottingham. I took people to London and collected them from various airports and ports. Not many Jamaicans had their own vehicles; those who worked at the pit often had motorbikes.

SPIRITUAL CONSCIOUSNESS

My father had two churches in Jamaica. I was brought up to be a 'church man' and I intended to get married. My mother gave me a Bible to take to England and marked scriptures in it for me to read. I started attending church regularly after the death of my mother. In 1959, I was 'saved' (confirmed) to become a committed Christian.

I then started my own church in the cellar of my house and held church services, sometimes with over eighty people attending. I made the baptism pool myself. It was a registered church but I could not marry people. I called it the 'Church of God Assembly'. This was one of the first black churches in Nottingham. Another was Park Hill on Derby Road, near Canning Circus, Nottingham. To join a Church of England church you had to make a request and get permission from parishioners. This made me feel uncomfortable so naturally, I found it so much easier to create my own church.

SOCIALISING

I never went to the Calypso Club, as I was not a 'sports man' (cricket lover). Occasionally, I went to the Sherwood Rooms (now the MGM nightclub), a popular entertainment venue on Greyfriar Gate. Ray Charles performed there one night in the 1970s - many young girls fainted on the ground! He sang, 'Take the chains from my heart and set me free'.

POINT OF NO RETURN

I originally intended to stay in the UK for three years to work and save, then return to Jamaica permanently. However, I have been back to Jamaica six times, most of the times for funerals: my mother, father, brother and my first wife. After having my children, making home improvements, and running a church, I had to be in England for my responsibilities and I was committed to 'family'.

Mr Western Vaccianna and Mrs Jane (née Anderson) Vaccianna, 2012 together at the Christian Centre, Nottingham.

Photo: Nottingham News Centre

CHAPTER 11

REFLECTIONS FROM JANE VACCIANNA 'MISS JOSEPH' FORMER BUSINESS OWNER AND HOMEMAKER

My name is Jane Morde Anderson. I married twice, first to a Mr Roxall Joseph and then to Mr Western Vaccianna in 1991. I am from Sandy Ground, Saint Catherine, Jamaica. My mother was Justina Anderson and she had seven children: six girls and one boy.

I arrived in England in July 1961, leaving behind my own business back home. In fact, I felt well-off in Jamaica as I owned and ran a grocers shop and bar. The shop did not have a name, it was just in an area called, 'Sandy Ground'. No plans were made to sell the business when I left Jamaica as it was my mother who took over the running of the shop in my absence.

THE JOURNEY TO ENGLAND
I came to England to be with my husband-to-be and our two children. We later sent the fare to my mother for our third child to join us.

The journey took six weeks on the boat. I was very sick for a stretch of about two weeks and had to visit the hospital on the boat. As we arrived in Southampton, my husband was there to meet me and we took the train to Nottingham. Since my husband worked on the railway, we got cheaper tickets as he was employed as a 'Shunter'.

INITIAL REACTIONS TO COMMUNAL LIVING
I was not excited about coming to England but because my husband was already here, I decided to come and support him. I did not bring much luggage with me nor did I bring a lot of money because I didn't have to, as I believed my husband would help me. Before I came, Roxall, my husband, had tried to purchase a two-bedroomed house. As the sale was not completed when I arrived, we had to rent accommodation for three weeks. We rented one room to live in with the children.

Elegance: Jane with child.   Photo: Courtesy of Jane Vaccianna

As we were living with other families in this large house, I didn't want to go downstairs to make a drink for the children because I felt uncomfortable surrounded by strangers. My children and I were always cold and I always had to keep them by the fire. I used to wait until my husband came home from work for company as I really was not used to living with different people in this way. Thankfully, we were able to move into our own house three weeks later. I offered one of the tenants a room in our house as this gesture enabled me to make friends and it helped somebody else.

Family first: Jane with first husband and the children.

Photo: Courtesy of Jane Vaccianna

Family ties: Jane with twins.

Photo: Courtesy of Jane Vaccianna

Island Beauty: Jane Vaccianna (neé Anderson)

Photo: Courtesy of Jane Vaccianna

PRESSURES

After a while, my husband began to change for the worst and was not nice and respectable to me after I had my five children. I found that I could not go out and socialise, as I wanted to. In Jamaica, I could close my shop on a Sunday and go to church but here, married and in England, I felt restricted and trapped. On the other hand, I was blessed to have a house and nice furniture. Unfortunately, when my husband got into financial trouble, he could not pay the mortgage so we had to leave our house.

- In memory of Jane Vaccianna who passed away February 12, 2014. -

CHAPTER 12

REFLECTIONS FROM LENA CURL GREGORY FORMER GENERAL (NOW CITY) HOSPITAL WORKER

I was born September 1st 1940 in Riversdale, St Catherine, Jamaica and grew up in Orange St, Kingston but my mother and brothers and sisters: Derek, Tony, Hyacinth, Enid and Catherine lived in Riversdale.

I went to St Anthony's Senior Catholic School in Kingston, Jamaica and did not attend college. As a teenager, I wanted to be a nurse. I always thought about it but the opportunity never came.

I found out about coming to England through my partner and future husband Donald Augustus Gregory (now deceased). We met in Riversdale, St Catherine, Jamaica. My sister Hyacinth orchestrated our meeting in Riversdale as she felt we were a good match. I had two sons for Everton Walker called Michael Walker and Howard Walker and then a son for Donald and named him Junior Donald Gregory.

My husband, was a farm worker and he saw a job advert in Jamaica for the Beeston Boiler Company off Queen's Road, Nottingham, wanting workers for their iron factory in Nottingham. Donald applied for employment and received an offer. He travelled to England in 1963. Donald later paid for my aeroplane ticket of £85 and I flew to England in 1965. Not a lot of Jamaicans left Jamaica by aeroplane as many went by boat so it felt special.

Donald saved up his wages from the Beeston Boiler Company and threw a 'pardoner' the way many Jamaicans and other West Indians used to save collectively. Many Jamaicans did not have bank accounts so grouped together and saved. Every month one of the group members would get a payout, enabling that person to purchase 'bigger things' like a deposit on a home, shop, travel tickets and so on.

Lena Gregory with Michael Walker, first son (neé McCormack), 1963. Photo: courtesy of Lena Gregory

MY ARRIVAL

I didn't bring much with me. I packed just a few pieces of clothing in one suitcase. Before I left Jamaica, I thought England was a nice place as many Jamaicans were talking about England and everybody wanted to go to get a job and earn money. I had no idea what I was going to do in England. No idea. I brought around two pounds with me, not much. Donald sent money for me before I left Jamaica, which was kind.

When I came off the aeroplane, the weather was cold and I saw big buildings: everywhere looked like factories. There were many white

Lena Gregory and second child, Howard Walker in 1964.
Courtesy of Lena Gregory

Multi-purpose living areas called 'home' at 8 Newstead Grove, 1968.
Photo: courtesy of Lena Gregory

people. I did not see many black people when we came off the aeroplane. Donald came to meet me at the airport with Oscar Robinson and I felt relieved seeing them waiting when I landed. Donald and I lived at 2 Heskey St, St Ann's in 1965, later moved to Burns St in 1967 and then 8 Newstead Grove in 1968 within the same vicinity. We rented one room as there were four rooms in the house.

Through some friends, I managed to find employment at Hickling & Pentecost, a lace dying, bleaching and finishing factory on Park Road, Lenton, now demolished and part of the site of the Cornerstone Church, Castle Boulevard. Myself and others went straight to the factory to seek work.

Once we became employees in the factory, we had to fold up the lace. I did not like the job very much as I only earned four or five pounds a week in wages, which was not a lot of money then. However, Donald earned thirteen pounds per week at Beeston Boilers. We used the money

to pay rent and continue dropping a 'pardoner' (saving). I had no time for hobbies as I simply worked to bring up the children.

MARRIAGE AND SOCIALISING
Donald and I got married on 27th March 1966 at Shakespeare Street Registry Office. Oscar Robinson was the Best Man and Vina his wife (deceased) was Maid of Honour. We had a party after at our rented room at 2 Heskey Walk. The wedding cake was extra special for us as I was the one who made it.

FINDING MY WAY
Fellow Jamaicans and friends helped me to find my way around the city. They showed me how to get to Nottingham City Centre and how to catch the bus. We used to buy bed spreads and bed linen from the Indian community. We bought Jamaican food from Mitchell's Grocery Store (now on Alfreton Road, Nottingham). He was one of the few Jamaican shop owners in Nottingham at this time.

Hyson Green Flats, 27 Bedford Walk, dressing up for a photograph, 1975.

Photo: courtesy of Lena Gregory

My next job was at the General Hospital in 1967, where I earned five pounds per week working in the restaurant. At the City Hospital, I worked as an Orderly and Catering Assistant until I retired aged 65, in 2005.

I lived at 12 Burns St when I was expecting my second child, Verna Gregory, born (at the General Hospital) 1st February 1967. We moved again to 8 Newstead Grove in 1968 where my daughters Flona (born 1st April, 1968) and Norma (10th June, 1969) were born at home. After this, we lived at 3 Bedford Walk on in Hyson Green Flats from 1973, where my last child Celia was born (31st May, 1973) until 1976 where we saved, managed to get a mortgage and bought a three bedroomed-house in Mapperley Plains, Nottinghamshire.

During the 1960s, I did not go anywhere at night: no clubs, pubs or house parties. We just made friends with who we lived with. I did not go to church when we first came to England. Music was my speciality: I enjoyed listening to Mick Jagger and Bob Marley who were the popular musical artists when I came to England.

Lena McCormack and Donald Gregory wedding day, 27th March 1966.   Courtesy of Lena Gregory

61

Content and at peace: Lena Gregory, aged 74.   Photo: Nottingham News Centre

LESSONS LEARNT

What I have learnt most from my forty-nine years in England is not to be aggressive. My only regret is that I never went into nursing. I would have liked the opportunity to train as a nurse as a Matron at the City Hospital said that I would have made a very good nurse. However, I could not because of the care and time needed to raise my children.

England has done a lot for me. I have learnt not to be ignorant or quick-tempered. When I was in Jamaica, every little thing used to upset me. Nottingham people have been alright. I have never been through any aggression with white or black people. England has done me well. I have bought my house in Mapperley and my children are successful in their different jobs, so I am happy.

CHAPTER 13

REFLECTIONS FROM CONSETTA WHITELEY 'MILLIE'
FORMER OFFICE WORKER AND SEAMSTRESS

My name is Consetta Elizabeth Whiteley (Millie) and I was born on the 3rd April, 1946. I came to England on 24th January 1964 when I was seventeen years old. In Jamaica, I was at Janetstone School an 'all in one' school (primary and senior school from aged six to sixteen) in Clarendon. At school, I enjoyed History, Geography and wanted to learn English. Young people knew about England through school. I was taught about our 'mother country' as Jamaica was ruled by England and I was taught to understand and learn that we were colonial subjects of England.

FAMILY MATTERS

I am one of eleven children: five girls and six boys. My mother, Mariam Miller married in 1926. I lived with my mother and found out about coming to England from my father George Oliver Miller who was already settled in Nottingham.

He sent for me and booked my flight. I did not need to bring a lot of money because he was already employed and ready to receive me. He was sixty years old when he came here. I asked him why he wanted to migrate for a new life at that age and he said that he had heard about England and wanted to see what it was like for himself. He sold many pieces of his land to raise money and planned to come to England for seven years. He worked at Radcliffe Power Station and later left to work on a building site.

TRAVEL ARRANGEMENTS

My teacher took me to 'Chin Yee's' Travel Service in bustling Kingston, Jamaica to get my travel tickets which cost £99. I remember when I took my passport picture, I combed my hair over my ears but my teacher said I could not do this and that I had to have every part of my face showing.

Consetta (Millie) aged 28.   Photo: courtesy of C Whiteley.

I left Kingston for London, Heathrow Airport. My suitcase contained an English grammar book called, *'First Aid in English'* to help me improve my spoken and written English.

My father was supposed to meet me at the airport. However, a few weeks before, 'Teddy Boys' beat him up whilst on his way back from work. When I saw him, his eyes were bruised and puffy. Due to his injuries, he wasn't able to meet me so I had to travel from London to Nottingham by myself. I had a rough time as I did not have a coat to protect me as my father was supposed to bring a coat and a cardigan for me. All I had on was a thin sage coloured suit. My body was shivering with cold and I was scared. When I

A mother's love, Millie aged 19, with son, Lloyd, in 1965.
Photo: courtesy of C. Whiteley

Party queens: Paulette Matthews, Millie (centre) aged 26 and Joan Davis at the Sherwood Rooms, 1971.
Photo: courtesy of C. Whiteley

asked for directions, one man tried to send me all the way to Manchester. A fight nearly broke out because somebody found out he was trying to put me on the wrong train. I finally got the right train from Victoria, London to Nottingham.

NOTTINGHAM IN THE 1960s

On my arrival at Nottingham Station, I got a taxi to 121 North Sherwood St and thought what a lot of factories because there was lots of smoke from the chimneys. After I woke up the next morning, someone called me and said look outside - snow! I was very excited.

My dad had rented a room because he was on his own and many Jamaican people and migrants in general, did not have the money to buy their own houses back then. However, Jamaicans coming from America could buy property because they had saved enough money through the opportunities of employment and better pay in America. I remember Mr Gayle, a Jamaican, who lived on Cranmer Street, had

quite a few houses and was able to rent rooms to many people in need.

My first job was on Victoria Road, off Haydn Road in Sherwood. This was factory work specialising in lace and other goods for Marks and Spencer. I folded up 'nighties' and slips (under skirts) and my salary was £3.69 per week. The 69p was for national insurance. I never saved anything because I had my dad helping me.

HOUSE PARTIES UNITED US

The people of Nottingham seemed quite friendly. I was not lonely because I had friends who had come from the same area in Jamaica. My father and family friends used to have house parties that brought everyone together in a relaxed atmosphere. In addition, I used to go to Birmingham to visit other people whilst my partner (and future husband) sometimes went to the Calypso Club on Byard Lane as well as and the Dungeon Club within the same vicinity.

Umbrella of happiness: Millie and husband, Alderman Whiteley.   Photo: courtesy of C. Whiteley

MARRIED LIFE

I got married aged 19, in 1966 in the Registry Office on Shakespeare Street. I remember it was a Tuesday. My husband and I did not have a wedding reception in the evening as my husband went straight back to work as he was on duty working nights. I am still waiting for my wedding reception after forty-eight years of marriage!

LESSONS IN LIFE

I have realised that no group of people is better than other – no matter how wealthy or economically challenged as we all have qualities that others might not have. I am grateful for my family; especially my children and I have no regrets. I would not want to live in Jamaica again because my family is here and I will never leave them.

Newstead Abbey, Nottinghamshire has links with Jamaica by way of its former owners, the Wildman family. It was Colonel Thomas Wildman (1787-1859) and family who inherited their fortune through wealth generated from the labour of over eight hundred enslaved Africans on their fifty-five acre sugar plantation called Quebec Estate in the parish of St Mary, north east Jamaica. Quebec Estate was next door to Frontier Plantation where Tacky, a Coromantee (Ghanaian) leader, led a slave rebellion on Easter Monday in 1760. Thomas Wildman purchased Newstead Abbey for around £90,000 in 1818 from romantic poet, Lord George Gordon Bryon (1788-1824).   Photo: Nottingham News Centre

A 'Slave Legacies' educational visit to Newstead Abbey, Nottinghamshire, organised by Lisa Robinson (bottom row, right) and team in 2014. .   Photo: Nottingham News Centre

Newstead Abbey, front view.   Photo: Nottingham News Centre

CHAPTER 14

REFLECTIONS FROM MARY JOHNSON
FORMER CARE HOME OWNER

Mary Burrell is my maiden name later changed to Mary Johnson through my marriage. I was born on the 29th May 1933 and left Jamaica aged twenty-four, originally growing up in Bartons, near Old Harbour in St Catherine, Jamaica. I have three brothers: James, Ethlene and Foster and two sisters: Martha and Eunice. I went to Barton's Elementary School aged seven, which was where my educational life started as it was believed by many that we did not go to school until we were aged seven in Jamaica. However, I now know the many started school aged five.

I left school aged fourteen (the leaving age was sixteen) and was married at nineteen years old, which was stupid. I had two children by 1957. I remember Rock and Roll music being popular in Jamaica when I was young but since I was a 'church person' (Christian) I wasn't really into that kind of music and discouraged from it.

My husband arrived in England, in 1956, and started saving by 'dropping his pardoner' so that within a year of getting his first draw (savings), he used that money to send for me.

I came to England in July, 1957. Jamaican were also finding work in United States because America's borders were 'open' then. Afterwards, we heard, through word of mouth, that England was inviting people to come and work. I had no professional skills and found work doing domestic and cleaning work. By way of work experience, I was employed by the Post Office whilst in Jamaica.

CHIN YEE'S' TRAVEL SERVICE, KINGSTON

My ticket was booked at 'Chin Yee's' Travel Service in Kingston, Jamaica as they sorted everyting out. I travelled by ship to England as

By the seaside: Mary dressed for a day trip by the sea. 1967　　　　Photo: courtesy of M Johnson.

I did not have the money to come by areoplane at £85.The boat ticket cost £75. My family could not find the £10 difference I needed for a shorter journey and I also needed to take some pocket money. I remember the ship was called the *Black Maria*. It sailed to Spain and there I bought a hat and a pair of sandals. They were so pretty.

I travelled with a group of people. To be honest, I was not excited about going to England because I left my two children behind and was worried about them. I packed clothes as well as some Jamaican food: some *bammy* (baked cassava) and 'coconut drops' (coconut sweet cake) in my hand luggage as snacks.

Mary Johnson (second right) off to church, smart dress required. 1963   Photo: courtesy of Mary Johnson

Well rested, Mary Johnson, aged 81.   Photo: Nottingham News Centre

HUNGER QUELLED

On arrival in England, I was extremely cold and shaking because I was wearing cotton, summer clothing. It was night time and I did not know where I was going. I got a train from Southampton to Northampton then to Midland (Nottingham) station and took a taxi to 15 Garnett Street, off Carlton Road, Nottingham and my husband was there to greet me. I travelled alone and was hungry. I remember a young woman on the train offering some of her sandwich to me. I was happy for the offer and said "yes". It was cheese and onion and it tasted so nice!

PARRAFIN HEATERS

My husband and I rented one room, with a bed and a paraffin heater lit in the middle of the room. The house had four rooms, which were all rented out. My husband bought me some warm clothes, a coat, warm vests, and warm underwear because I kept shaking and shivering because of the cold weather.

HIGH EXPECTATIONS AND AMBITIONS

When I came to England, I wanted to go to college but had no chance because of the children, I simply had to look after them and I was expecting another child in 1958.

I managed to go to evening classes, aged twenty-five, at the school on the corner of Bentick Road, Hyson Green. Thankfully, the course was free as I had little money. There, I learnt to sew and to do overlocking. I became a machinist and later found work in Basford, sorting out old rags. However, I left soon after as I couldn't take this sort of job any more and found employement as a machinist in 1959, behind the Shipstone Building in Basford, Nottingham.

I really wanted to work in the hospital as I always loved caring for people. So I applied lots of times but could not get through since so many others were also applying for hospital jobs.

It was not until during the 1970s that I got a job at the Nottingham City Hospital as an Auxiliary

Councillor Eunice Campbell (centre) with the Sheriff of Nottingham, Jackie Morris (left) and guest launch Nottingham's Older Citizen's Charter at the Council House on Senior Citizens Day, 1st October 2014. Photo: Nottingham News Centre

Nurse. I loved working there and stayed until I retired aged fifty five.

BUSINESS IDEAS AND SELF EMPLOYMENT
I decided to start my own business in partnership with two other ladies in 1988. We started our own business, a rest home for the elderly in West Bridgeford called, 'Care Plus Rest Home'. We were quite succesful but we later sold the business and retired completely in the 1990s. I enjoyed my work, caring for the elderly.

MEMORIES OF NOTTINGHAM'S RIOTS
I remember two race riots: one in St Ann's 1958 and the other in Hyson Green in 1981. I had two sons and always told them to be in no later than nine at night. On the day of the 1981 riots, only one of my sons came home on time. In the morning, we did not know where my son was. A neighbour said I should ring the police station. I rang the police and fortunately was allowed to speak to my

son. I can remember hearing a distraught pitch in his voice from crying. When I spoke to him he said that he was not involved in the troubles but went to look at what was happening. He ended up running towards Hyson Green. Naturally, he got caught up with the crowd and was arrested. I had to go to the Guildhall to try to find a solicitor. Thankfully, my son came out of the police cell and got a good talking to. I will never forget that.

FINAL THOUGHTS OF THANSKGIVING
I am grateful for my children, they have had a good education and are all doing very well. I have been happy here in England and I have only been back to Jamaica twice. Jamaica is too rough for me, I cannot take it out there, I was shaking when I returned from there on my last trip. I know there is nothing there for me now, England is my home.

Proposal for the National Pensioners' Convention Dignity Code, presented in Nottingham. Photo: Nottingham News Centre

Jamaican senior citizens enjoy a day at the Council House, Nottingham. Photo: Nottingham News Centre

SECTION 2

JAMAICANS IN NOTTINGHAM

A Collection of Narratives and Reflections of the Present

CHAPTER 15

ARTICLE: 'MERLITA BRYAN SHERIFF OF NOTTINGHAM VISITS THE ACNA CENTRE TO CELEBRATE HER INAUGURATION'

Crowds celebrate with Arnold Wright (left) Sheriff Merlita Bryan, Professor Cecile Wright and George Powe (right) a first for Nottingham: a Jamaican born black, female Sheriff of Nottingham, August 2012.

Photo: Nottingham News Centre

Councillor Merlita Bryan celebrated her inauguration as Sheriff of Nottingham at the Afro-Caribbean Artistic Centre (ACNA) on Saturday 27h July 2012. Over two hundred members of the community warmly welcomed the first Jamaican, female Sheriff of Nottingham. Merlita greeted well-wishers and shared her experiences following a three-course dinner prepared by the Hummingbird Caterers. Merlita later unveiled her official portrait, in Mayoral dress standing in the Council House Cambers, on the wall of ACNA Centre reception area. Her photograph joins other portraits featuring the likes of George Leigh, George Powe, Simon Powell, Lyn Gilzean, Des Wilson, Tony Robinson and others who have made significant differences to improve conditions experienced within the community.

Professor Cecile Wright, from Nottingham University, opened the reception with a dedication to the life and community work achieved by Councillor Bryan since 1989. Bryan in response said: "My role is an opportunity to do things for the community." She added, "I hope to help encourage young people to get involved in politics," and explained that her role would help promote better community relations within the city.

Article originally written by Norma Gregory and sent to the Nottingham Evening Post on 30th July 2012. Summarised and printed (including photograph) by the Nottingham Evening Post, 4th August 2012.

Reference courtesy of Nottingham Evening Post

CHAPTER 16

SPEECH BY GEORGE POWE
GIVEN AT THE ANCA CENTRE, 27TH JULY, 2012

'CELEBRATION OF MERLITA BRYAN'S ACHIEVEMENT OF BEING THE FIRST AFRICAN CARIBBEAN WOMAN TO BECOME SHERIFF OF NOTTINGHAM'
"Good evening,

I would like to welcome Merlita Bryan on this important occasion, a celebration of the fact that she is the first African Caribbean, Jamaican woman to become the Sheriff of Nottingham. I wonder what Robin Hood would have thought of this?

As legend accords, Robin Hood was working hard to rob the rich to give to the poor, then it would seem quite a prime example to strive towards fundamentals of equality; better still, a model for the message I have for you!

As someone who knows what drives the host community, and those of us who have settled here, as well as the people of Jamaica, I know many women have been through struggles to achieve equality in terms of class, race, sex, education, social standing and opportunity in general. The pace of change is different in each element. However, the pattern basically remain the same, direct action, political and social campaigns, discussion, debates and sometimes legislation.

It is always difficult for one group of people to put aside feelings of discrimination, which have been implanted in them by their upbringing and cultural heritage. The area which has been most fraught and on which there has been the most conflict within these communities as well as between them, is discrimination against women.

In Jamaica, as well as in the host community and ethnic minority communities in this country, many men find it difficult to afford women the fullness of respect and dignity they so richly deserve. It is probably true to say that, there have been more white people campaigning for

Robin Hood statue, Nottingham Castle.
Photo: Nottingham News Centre

the rights of black people than the number of men of any group campaigning for women's rights.

We all need to look at this with reference to the reason for the celebration this evening. It is great to have an African Caribbean Sheriff of Nottingham, as we have had a Sheriff from our community in the past. His name is Tony Robinson. Today fate, albeit destiny, has allowed a women to take the mantle we celebrate today.

Let us have some applause here for what Merlita has achieved. However, let us not forget that these struggles are on-going. African Caribbean people, men and women, are under-represented in positions of power and influence.

Nottingham Council House officially opened in 1929.

Photo: Nottingham News Centre

This must be addressed.

The younger generation of African Caribbean young people, who have to deal with more subtle kinds of discrimination, need to join with their elders to combat this, the elders in turn reaching out to their offspring youth in a spirit of co-operation.

I hope that within my lifetime, there will be an upsurge in the numbers of African Caribbean people who can celebrate their achievements with pride, thereby moving into positions of honour.

If this happens and someone else from our community achieves as in the case of Merlita, let us give thanks for the notion that barriers to race, class and caste will at last be coming down in favour of the forces of upward social mobility, which must be celebrated. I would like to propose that Lloyd Burrell the present Chair of ACNA, ensures that a written record of Merlita's political and social achievements be catalogued and made available for future reference for all the community and beyond.

Finally, I would like to finish by telling you about a remarkable role model for African Caribbean women in particular. During the 1960s, there was a Trinidadian woman who became famous for her selfless campaigning for the rights of African Caribbean people. She went to the USA and joined the Communist Party, who at the time, were actively involved in our struggles as a people. Her name was Claudia Jones.

Her writings, speeches and agitation all helping to raise consciousness. The Americans deported her to England, not Trinidad. She tried to visit Jamaica, but was denied access because of her own political stance. She lived here until she died, always politically active and was known as the mother of the Notting Hill Carnival. Her name was the great Claudia Jones.

If you want to know more about her, do some research. Thank you for listening."

Included with kind permission from Mr George Powe on the 27th July 2012.

In memory of Mr George Powe who passed away on 9th September 2013.

Courtesy of Jill Westby, widow of George Powe.

CHAPTER 17

MAYOR MAGNIFICENT!
REFLECTIONS FROM... COUNCILLOR MERLITA BRYAN
FORMER LORD MAYOR OF NOTTINGHAM

Councillor Merlita Bryan is a formidable woman of distinction and direction. As Lord Mayor of Nottingham (2013-2014), the most senior civic duty in the city, she has much to be proud of; by carrying out the ceremonial role dating back to 1284, with Roger de Crophill as the first on record. Now records have changed through Merlita Bryan, who for twelve months, from May 2013 to May 2014, will serve in the capacity of Lord Mayor for a community she has lived and worked in ever since she came here as a child, aged eleven, from Jamaica in 1962.

Merlita is one of many success stories in the history of Nottingham not only as a role model for women locally, nationally and internationally but also as a leader through her effort and spirit to improve the city and the lives of its citizens.

I had the privilege of spending time with Merlita, in chambers at the Nottingham City Council House, to find out how this important and life changing the role has impacted on her life, her hopes, aspirations, priorities and vision for the development of the city during her tenure as Lord Mayor.

Councillor Merlita Bryan opens the Nottingham Carnival 2013.   Photo: Nottingham News Centre

NG: As the first African Caribbean, female Lord Mayor of Nottingham, how has your background influenced your life's journey and current commitment to public life as first citizen, Lord Mayor of Nottingham?

M.B: I was born in St Thomas, Jamaica, of which I am very proud thereafter arriving in England in 1962 to join my parents. My dad came here first to join his sister, then my mum followed. I came here when I was very young, went to school, had various jobs and raised my children. However, I thought there was more to life than what I was doing. Later and from my Trade Union background,

I was encouraged to go into local government and after succeeding at the polls I became a Councillor. I realised then, that this was an opportunity to try to do something for my community where I live. The rest is history!

NG: When and how did you become the Lord Mayor of Nottingham?

MB: I was elected as Lord Mayor of Nottingham in March 2013 and the full induction was completed

Lord Mayor of Nottingham Merlita Bryan and Lady Mayoress, daughter Sharon Bryan.

Photo: courtesy of Nottingham City council

Celebrating Shiefton Youth Group & Supplementary School's 30th Anniversary, Merlita Bryan with host Angela Reid has time to support young people in Nottingham.

Photo: Nottingham News Centre

20th May 2013. Before this post, I was Sheriff of Nottingham from 2012 to 2013. The election process is carried out annually from within the Council. Nominations are made, which require a second recommendation. It is then put to a vote by Council members thereafter the Mayor is elected.

N.G: What does the role of Lord Mayor mean to you?

M.B: For me and my family, it is a big achievement. I would never ever have thought for one moment that I would be the Lord Mayor of Nottingham.

N.G: How has the community responded to the first African Caribbean woman Mayor of Nottingham?

M.B: The warm embrace I have experienced from the whole community has been phenomenal. I have had women say how uplifted and motivated they feel. In particular, the African Caribbean community has been fantastic and very supportive.

N.G: How do you think the role of Lord Mayor will help to improve the Nottingham community?

M.B: The Lord Mayor is the first citizen of Nottingham and is a Civic role to help promote the city. The role is to host visitors to the city, like the royal family and other dignitaries and Heads of State. Within the community, the Lord Mayor gets invited to open new businesses, schools or charity events and to deliver speeches. It is a big thing for the city to have a Lord Mayor, to represent and speak on behalf of the city. If individuals are lucky enough to get into a responsible role, it is not just for you – you should do it to embrace or enhance somebody else.

N.G: How can businesses be improved in the city of Nottingham?

M.B: For businesses to improve, we need to talk collectively and generate action. We need to speak to employers and community organisations and work with the Council to try to improve things. I know we are in recession at the moment but on a confident note, I feel things will get better in the future. We need to mobilize our youngsters to help themselves, pointing them in the right direction. It is very hard out there; we have been teenagers ourselves. Back in the day, it was not as hard as it is now - *we* thought it was difficult back then. We have to try and work with our youngsters to inspire them towards career paths that are viable and fulfilling.

N.G: What are your views on employment and self-employment within the Nottingham community?

M.B: We need to oil the wheels of self-help projects and training initiatives as well as encouraging big businesses to employ young people. The Council is doing a lot of apprentice schemes. Nowadays, every organisation wants somebody who is qualified but you can't get qualified unless you have a chance. Not everybody will leave school with bachelor's degrees. If you don't have a degree, it doesn't mean that you are not intelligent and you can't learn. We are missing a section of society who is going to be left behind all the time. We need to look at encouraging employers to take young people on straight from school. We need to bring back career advisers into schools.

N.G: What are your priorities as Lord Mayor of Nottingham?

M.B: Young people. I am passionate about the role young people will play in the future. Whenever I look at a young person, I see tomorrow's Lord Mayor, I see tomorrow's Member of Parliament or the next Prime Minister. I will work with anybody in order to steer our young people on track for tomorrow's world. For me, if being the Lord Mayor of Nottingham makes young people think, "I can achieve something, I can do that," that's what it's all about.

If the role helps to make youngsters feel they are not trapped, but can aspire and go for gold and do something, then that is what my work as Mayor

is for. Giving somebody else aspiration in the community and beyond, that's what it's all about, regardless of gender, race, status or beliefs. It is the belief that somebody from an ordinary, working background, like me, can achieve. That is how I hope the role will help people.

N.G: Describe a typical day as Lord Mayor of Nottingham.

M.B: It varies. In one day, I might have two, three or four civic engagements. I might have Council meetings, an interview with the press, a visit or a citizenship ceremony to welcome new British citizens to Nottingham.

N.G: How can the public help you in your duties over the year as Lord Mayor?

M.B: If organisations need help promoting what they are doing in the community, I am very happy to come along to support the event. Get in touch with the Civic Office through the Nottingham City Council's website, summarize the event and how my role could help your community-focused event.

Nottingham is a beautiful part of the East Midlands region and if we want to promote the city, we need to work together because this is where we are and we are not going to go anywhere else. Along with the Sheriff of Nottingham, I will try to support organisations and individuals who promote and highlight the good work achieved in our city.

©Norma Gregory
Written by Norma Gregory.
First published in *Mojatu Magazine*, Nottingham, Issue M009.
Courtesy of Mojatu Magazine.

Shiefton logo

Wisdom and a blessing, Merlita Bryan.

Photo: Nottingham News Centre

CHAPTER 18

ARTICLE: JULIUS GARVEY, SON OF JAMAICAN NATIONAL HERO VISITS NOTTINGHAM

Jacqueline Lockhart (left), Dr Julius Garvey, Linda Wright, Leslie Ayoola and Gwendoline Darby.

Photo: Nottingham News Centre

Dr Julius Mosiah Garvey's visit to Nottingham, on Friday 4th October 2013, was a triumphant occasion for hundreds of people in Nottingham to witness the presence of the son of the late Honourable Marcus Mosiah Garvey (1887-1940), the Jamaican orator, businessman, writer and Pan-Africanist. Julius Garvey now aged eighty, a New York based vascular surgeon, made a five-day tour of the UK visiting Birmingham, London, Manchester and Nottingham.

The visit was organized by the Jamaican High Commission with the help of Desmond Jaddoo,

a Birmingham based community activist who believed that the opportunity to see and hear the opinions of a living offspring of Garvey was not to be missed.

Welcomed with honours at Nottingham City Council House by the Lord Mayor of Nottingham, Councillor Merlita Bryan, Garvey was guest of honour at a Caribbean lunch with local community leaders and politicians.

He met a large group of Caribbean elders at the Marcus Garvey Centre based at the former Raleigh Bicycles Factory on Lenton Boulevard

Sheriff of Nottingham, Cllr Ian Malcolm (left) and guest with Julius Garvey and Merlita Bryan. Photo: Nottingham News Centre

before moving on to greet students and academics at Nottingham Trent University spending time to offer a lecture at the Students' Union.

His final stop was made at the Afro-Caribbean Nationals Artistic Centre (ACNA) where he was greeted with a drum call and rapturous applause from over two hundred people from Nottingham's Caribbean community.

Julius Garvey spoke of the potential of the African people manifested through the arts, music, religion, medicine, science, literature and sports. He spoke about his father's ability to challenge ideology in order to make the changes that he did. Garvey stated: "Those who have fought for our liberation and opened doors, some of them have passed on. Some of us are not exercising the freedoms we have. We have not found our voice or thought about others who have not gone through. We cannot simply go through the doors and join the system that exists. Create your own system." He added: "We cannot replace nature with technology as we have come out of nature. What has formed us, is the creative elements of the universe, a

representation of what some of us call God. We are destroying our homes and then we are saying we are homeless. It doesn't make sense."

Garvey concluded the evening at ACNA by answering questions from the packed audience concerning African participation in the Commonwealth, how Garveyism ideology can relate to young Africans plus, his earliest and fondest memories of his father.

©Norma Gregory
Written by Norma Gregory.

First published in *Mojatu Magazine*, Nottingham, Issue M011. Courtesy of *Mojatu Magazine*.

Dr Julius Garvey speaks of father's legacy at the ACNA Centre 4th October 2013. Photo: Nottingham News Centre

Norma Gregory as Editor of Mojatu Magazine with Julius Garvey. Photo: Nottingham News Centre

Crowds await the arrival of Julius Garvey to the ACNA Centre, 4th October 2013. Photo: Nottingham News Centre

Merlita Bryan welcomes Dr Julius Garvey to Nottingham, October 2013.

Photo: Nottingham News Centre

CHAPTER 19

DIVA DIVINE!
REFLECTIONS FROM REVEREND CANON EVE PITTS
CHURCH OF ENGLAND MINISTER

Reverend Canon Eve Pitts is a passionate preacher and pioneer in England's church history. She is known for her distinctive hairstyle, her humour, honesty in her sermons and passion for music and the arts.

I met with Reverend Pitts at her mother's home in Nottingham, to hear her views on the notion of a female Archbishop of Canterbury, her thoughts on feminine beauty, keeping healthy and her spiritual walk with God.

As the first black woman ordained as a Deacon in the Church of England (C of E) in 1992 and ordained as Reverend in 1994, Reverend Canon Pitts, aged 62, is well-known for her passionate speaking, fearless confidence and unmistakable hairstyle.

Born 1952 in May Pen, Jamaica, Reverend Pitts came to Nottingham, aged six. She grew up with love and support from her family and found the church leadership her 'calling'.

In 1988, she attended the acclaimed Queen's Foundation, Birmingham, founded in 1828, studying ecumenical theological education. She saw this as a preparation for her ministerial life in the C of E. She leads her parish by faith and commitment at Holy Trinity Church, Birchfield, Birmingham and frequently returns to Nottingham for weddings, funerals and other church commitments.

CHURCH
NG: Do you enjoy being a Reverend Canon?

EP: I love being a Reverend. I feel blessed! I love being able to communicate and use the gifts that God has given to me. I love people and I love being around people. I am passionate about making a difference in the community, to help to bring good changes.

Reverend Pitts, a blessed woman of the cloth.
Photo: Keith Steele Photography

Mansfield Road Baptist Church, where many church services for the Jamaican and West Indian community are held.

Photo: Nottingham News Centre

NG: You were the first female of African Caribbean descent and of Jamaican heritage ordained by the C of E. How do you feel about this?

EP: It was challenging being the first black Ordinate because I had to struggle against the Church turning me into a 'trophy'. I had to face issues of racism and sexism, which sadly is rampant in the Church and in society today. I think I got through unscathed - through my confidence and refusal to countenance it.

NG: What are your views on the possibility of a female Archbishop of Canterbury?

EP: I think we need to be in a position where the Church of England has female bishops first! They are still dragging their feet on the subject. I think this a great shame because we have many other things we need to do and should be doing about the world. As an institution, the Church is privileged enough to be in a position to make radical choices

about how we cope with the realities of our world and climate in which we live. At times, the Church is too timid. If the Church cannot be courageous enough to ordain women as priests, I don't see how it will have the courage to face ecological issues, economic or political problems. If the Church is not dealing with smaller issues, how can it respond to the unanswered questions that people ask like, "What is the Church for?"

NG: How would you describe your spiritual walk with God?

EP: Fierce. I don't find my walk with God easy. I find people who seem to walk through Christianity without difficultly or moments of doubt as bizarre. When the world around us is in such a terrible state, it is very difficult to believe that you can go through a Christian life and not ask, "Where are you God?" I don't always find being a Christian easy - I make no apology for that. For me, faith doesn't come easy.

NG: You are known for your sense of humour when preaching. Is humour important?

EP: I didn't even realise I was funny! Increasingly, over the years, people say to me, "Why don't you go on the stage?" "Well, I am!" I say. The pulpit is a kind of 'stage'. I inherited my sense of humour and wit from my father. A sense of humour is a great gift to have, especially in my work. It is a survival strategy and can help to punctuate difficult situations in life.

NG: What would you advocate to the youth of today?

EP: Self-respect. I feel somehow that we have lost something and we need to identify it and get it back. I would encourage our young to read more because there is a depth of ignorance that is intolerable partly to blame by an education system, which has let us down.

NG: What three things would you change in society?

EP: I think society needs to discover a new depth in spirituality. We need quietness and space to think and to rediscover the meaning of community. In society, there is the culture of, 'it's me and me alone'. I think this behaviour and ideology has done terrible harm to us.

NG: What are your first thoughts in the morning and last thing at night?

EP: First thing in the morning, I start with silence. I sit quietly and don't speak to anyone to get in touch with my own heart. This sets me up for the day and allows me to hear God. Without this quiet devotion in the morning, I find my day can become dysfunctional. I like to recite Psalms 51 at night.

BEAUTY AND HEALTH
NG: You wear your hair very short. What sort of comments have you had about your hairstyle?

EP: I have always worn my hair short. I feel beautiful with my hair short. It is a statement of confidence and

Spiritual sense, a regular minister of Jamaican funerals and weddings in Nottingham, Birmingham and beyond.
Photo: Keith Steele Photography

who I am as a black woman, how I see myself and my place in the world.

NG: What do you do to maintain good health?

EP: I walk a lot and choose not to drive because I like the idea of my feet touching the earth daily. It is how I pray and connect with God through the physical earth. When I abandoned my car ten years ago, that was a deliberate strategy to help me connect with people. I believe that God creates us for health. I ask God to give me health and in return I will do everything I can to make a difference to the community I serve. That's the deal!

NG: Are you house-proud?

EP: I like where I live to look good as long as I don't have to become a slave to my home. I like peaceful environments and I don't like chaos so my homes, in Nottingham and Birmingham are orderly I think! If your environment is chaotic, then it is highly likely that your life will be chaotic too.

Fearless, Reverend Eve Pitts.   Photo: Nottingham News Centre

SPIRITUALITY

NG: What is your most treasured possession?

EP: My three children are very precious to me but my most treasured possessions are my books. I love the novels, A *Suitable Boy* by Vicram Seth, *Small Island* by Angela Levy and *Invisible Man* by Ralph Ellison as well as any book by Toni Morrison.

NG: When are you happiest?

EP: I am happiest when I am preaching because it is my gift. I love preaching, as I love words, verbal communication and connecting with human beings.

NG: What three things does your congregation not know about you?

EP: My congregation probably don't know that I am a very good dancer. As Christians, we feel that we are not allowed to show or admit our sexual nature. I am a very sensual woman and I get annoyed when people want to put me in a box and shut away my sensuality and pretend that I am a one-dimensional human being who is a Christian and nothing more. I am much more than that. I am a Christian, yes in all its beauty. I love fashion and beautiful clothes. I enjoy reading and writing poetry as well.

NG: What do you think your legacy will be?

EP: I am not sure I will have one, as it is not something I think about. However, I hope I leave a legacy of love, as love is transformative.

NG: Do you have a personal motto?

EP: I can - because God says I can!

©Norma Gregory
Written by Norma Gregory.

First published in *Mojatu Magazine* Nottingham, Issue M011. Courtesy of *Mojatu Magazine*.

CHAPTER 20

REFLECTIONS FROM... BYRON WILLIAMS BUSINESSMAN AND OWNER OF WILLIAMS' BARBER SHOP, RADFORD

Sporting a crisp white, short-sleeved shirt and a cheeky smile, Byron Williams, owner of *Williams' Barber Shop* situated on Peveril Street, Nottingham, dusts off his well-worn black barber's chair to welcome the next client who has been patiently waiting and in no rush to leave. *'Service with a smile'* is the shop's motto on entering and clearly the principle by which Byron lives and serves his customers.

Byron decided to start his own business in February 2009 as he wanted to gain a sense of independence and the financial gains of being self-employed, managing his work schedule as well as the time needed to collect his children from school. He trained in barbering at the Kingston School of Cosmetology, Jamaica and then learnt his trade further through observation and assistance from fellow barbers who helped each other out by sharing new barbering skills picked up from New York. "As kids growing up, we took it on ourselves to teach each other and be self-sufficient," said Byron, taking a moment to recollect his early childhood experiences in Jamaica before coming to the UK in 2006.

He was born in the St Ann District (towards the north of Jamaica) but grew up in the Parish of Manchester, Jamaica. Now a fit (he would consider himself so) man of forty-four. "I can't say I grew up in any one place. I grew up all over Jamaica because I have a moving mentality - I can't stay in one place for too long! This was much to do with my mother who moved from Trelawny to Manchester, then to Kingston. So yes, it was when I arrived in Kingston that thoughts of barbering entered my mind, aged twenty. I was having to leap-frog from address to address as my father passed away in my early teens."

Byron describes the career of barbering as very competitive and hard work. His main challenge

Byron Williams owner of Williams' Barber Shop, Radford.
Photo: Nottingham News Centre

was his attempt to overcome certain barriers and stereotypes for black male business owners as he is based in Radford, Nottingham. "It is pointless going into some areas like Mapperley or West Bridgford to ply our trade. You won't find people drive from West Bridgford to Radford for a haircut! White people would prefer to go to an Indian barber for a haircut. They don't want to come to a person of African descent for a haircut. Some think we can't do it. Yes we can! We can do it. I can do any hair from any nation. Doing business in Radford has its pluses but also minuses as well," he says.

Byron always has advice and time for young people who frequent his barbershop for time out to share ideas for their latest hair designs. "As I have young lads myself, some young men who come to my barbershop think there is nowhere to go and nothing to do. I found myself in the capacity of a

Skillful, musical youth.   Photo: Nottingham News Centre

counsellor for these young guys. It wasn't until I started to interact with them that I realized they are seeing things as hopeless. One young guy, whilst communicating his concerns, said if things continued like this he would hang himself, which is really sad. I tried to speak to him and let him know it's not all about *him*. That he had family and siblings. I try to guide them and say life is not what you see; it is what you make of it. I try to give words of encouragement. Guys come from Aspley and Broxtowe areas purely for advice and for a place to relax for a while," says Byron with a hint of sadness permeating his memory.

He went on to state that, "The British notion of culture can sometimes stereotype young guys, all because of the economic situation that is leading people into a state of deprivation. For example, if you look at the whole area of Radford, you can see deprivation creeping in again. Some shops are finding it hard in the city centre to make a profit because of shoplifting. People go into town to just take things if they don't have a job. What do you do? Sometimes the troubles are self-inflicted. I have had customers come up and say they want a haircut

for £5 when my hair cut costs £8. I can do my part to help but the next time he will be back and want a haircut for £6. If I don't do it for £6, he might do something he regrets. What can I do?

If you want to start your own business, go for it and work hard at it. Prepare to build your mind up to succeed. Because of the economic situation right now, there is a chance of failure unless you plan and work hard for success. If you fail it is not my fault - blame it on the economy!" says Bryon with his Jamaican sense of humour shining through his warm nature.

When asked if he exercises his vote, Byron said: "Yes, I do because in Jamaica I was a Labour (Party) man. There is something about the Labour Party that I find intriguing."

For the future, Bryon envisions hope. "Without hope there will be no opportunity for our young people. If we can steer youth towards opportunity, we will make them better people. A youth doesn't want to feel insecure, whether financially, spiritually, socially, mentally or psychologically. If we can engender hope for the future for them, that would be our greatest goal.

I would like to see job opportunities. I would like to see adults becoming more proactive in the sense of enforcing certain disciplines and giving more guidance. When I see the *yout dem* pacing up and down with drop-down pants and bent up faces and can't even say hello, it makes my heart ache. We have a culture of saying leave it alone or it doesn't concern me. When challenged, the youth say, 'my dad never told me off before so why are you telling me off? My dad never listens to me or even tries to understand what I'm going through," is what some of *de yout dem* will often say. My message to the *yout dem* is simple: Respect yourself and respect the elders. If you have a youth growing up, who does not care about himself, he won't care about you neither," he said. Byron Williams, a man with a passion for barbering and for supporting the youth in preparing for the future.

©Norma Gregory
Written by Norma Gregory.

First published in *Mojatu Magazine*, Issue M009. Courtesy of *Mojatu Magazine.*

CHAPTER 21

NARRATIVES AND REFLECTIONS FROM NORMA JACQUELINE GREGORY, AUTHOR

8 Newstead Grove, Nottingham. My place of birth.
Photo: Nottingham News Centre

A typical children's group photo taken by Mr Brown Photographer, Burns St 1972. Courtesy of Lena Gregory

I was born at home at 8 Newstead Grove, Nottingham in 1969, the fourth of five children of Lena and Donald Gregory natives of St Catherine, Jamaica. We moved to 3 Bedford Walk in the Hyson Green Flats on Radford Road (now demolished, with Asda on the huge site) and resided here from 1973 to 1976. My mother had no desire to remain at the Flats due to crowded living conditions and our general safety and sought to obtain a mortgage from the Halifax Building Society to purchase a house somewhere else. I remember a removal van taking our belongings and 1960s furniture to Mapperley, Nottinghamshire in the October of 1976.

I attended Scotholme Primary School (1974-1976) Hyson Green, Mapperley Plains Primary School (1976-1980) and Frank Wheldon Comprehensive School and Sixth Form (1980-1986) in Carlton, Nottinghamshire. I remember, on the way home from school, I would often drop into Mapperley Library to explore the multitude of books and topics of interest in the Children's Library on the first floor.

I recall my schooling was not filled with the happiest of memories except for my participation in most of the sports clubs and sports teams. My attendance at lunchtime and after school clubs in craft, chess and gardening was frequent at primary school plus netball, badminton, rounders, athletics and any other sport where I could run fast and use my shoulder strength (except cross country and swimming) at secondary school.

Being encouraged by teachers to do well at sport, for a child of African Caribbean descent, was common in the 1970s and 1980s as well as being placed in the bottom groups for English and Maths 'as black children were no good at English' a premise I and many others were taught to believe at that time.

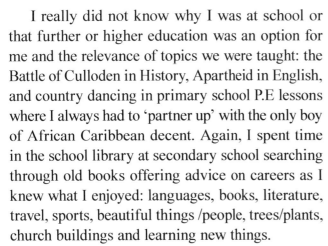

Dressed to attend a wedding, 1973.

Courtesy of Lena Gregory

Christmas time in the Hyson Green Flats, 1975.

Courtesy of Lena Gregory

I really did not know why I was at school or that further or higher education was an option for me and the relevance of topics we were taught: the Battle of Culloden in History, Apartheid in English, and country dancing in primary school P.E lessons where I always had to 'partner up' with the only boy of African Caribbean decent. Again, I spent time in the school library at secondary school searching through old books offering advice on careers as I knew what I enjoyed: languages, books, literature, travel, sports, beautiful things /people, trees/plants, church buildings and learning new things.

My source of income came from 10p a week pocket money from my father (on a Friday 6pm), my newspaper delivery ('paper round') after school when I was eleven years old and my Saturday job at Saxone Shoes on the corner of Exchange Walk from aged fourteen to seventeen working and then socialising with my mates Natalie Fenton, Julie James and Julie White: drinking, night-clubbing at 'Dr Zhivago's' and hanging out in various parks. What a life!

HIT THE ROAD JACQ: MY MOVE TO LONDON

After finishing secondary school in 1985 and an additional year wasted in sixth form, spent gambling and playing cards trying to win my five pence bus fare home, I lacked direction and professional ambition (except for modelling which was not a 'job').

I entered the national Youth Training programme called the 'YTS Scheme,' where I worked for a firm (Jessops department store) full-time in the hosiery department and got paid £27.30 on a Friday each week. Following this, I worked at Warehouse, a women's clothing store before leaving Nottingham in September 1987, aged 18 to move to London to pursue a career in fashion modelling (starting in Nottingham through Ukaidi youth projects in Marple Square), attending the London College of Fashion for less than one year.

This career option did not materialise as desired at the time as my love of chocolate combined with my Saturday job in the Luxury Chocolates Food

School uniform annual mug shot, 1981.

Courtesy of Lena Gregory

School Sports Day, 1983.

Courtesy of Lena Gregory

Hall at Harrods do not help the required figure for modelling in the late 1980s. I left my college course early, due to weight-associated anxieties combined with feelings of isolation.

Following this, I explored a variety of employment avenues in order to pay rent and live in the capital city, London. I worked in Harrods Ladies Scarves department and later offered an opportunity (and more pay) to become one of the first female security guards at Harrods, Knightsbridge and thus the first African Caribbean female security guard. My work in the security department was often repetitive and mundane on the shop floor with excitement thrown in through the occasion shoplifter and frequent pick-pockets operating in gangs in the store. After work, staff hosted parties in Brompton Place and shared stories of their day at work.

However, through these feelings of boredom and desire to learn more and do more began my destiny of re-education. I began to read more: newspapers and biographies, which relit my thirst for knowledge and understanding through books. So in 1994, I decided to return to study at evening classes at the College of South West London, resitting GCSE examinations in English and French, two subjects I loved from school but never excelled in. This renewed passion for reading and writing and a flame lit for learning as much as I could, urged me to return to full-time education but this time on my terms and in more control to learn what I needed to learn. I held a farewell celebration at Harrods with all the staff and management in the Security department and resigned from my job in August 1994.

SEEKING A 'RE-EDUCATION'

From this point in my life, I started to believe and understand that everyone had a human right to pursue an active and creative life, whether through formal or informal educational routes towards financial and personal independence. Therefore, early in 1994 and with that positive mindset, I decided to write a four-page letter

Modelling days, 1988.   Charles Sagoe Photography

I thoroughly enjoyed by studies at St Mary's and found myself studying as much as the day could allow in the college library; in the 18th century Walpole House, a castle like mansion with turrets, situated in the grounds of St Mary's or in my room on the beautiful and tranquil campus. My rest times were spent in the student bar and in the neighbouring town of Richmond with student friends and lecturers, many of whom I still keep in contact with today. Due to hard work, studying throughout the day and night and holiday periods; a commitment to my love of literature and desire to listen and learn, I was honoured with an upper second-class degree (2:1) in 1999 at my graduation ceremony at Westminster Cathedral in Victoria, London. I reflect on the happiest of memories gained from St Mary's and consider my experience as pivotal and life-changing in my ensuing professional and personal journey, for which I am forever grateful to all those who helped along the way.

PREPARING FOR LIFE IN LITERACY

Leaving St. Mary's in 1999 and over subsequent months, my feelings of elation began to fade and a few months doubt and lack of direction hit me hard and forced me to spend a week in silent retreat (as well as the time to write and to think about my future), at St Mary's Convent in Massingham, Norfork. Soon after my return home to my flat in Stoke Newington, North London, I made an application to the Millennium Commission, funded by the National Lottery, to fund a community project interviewing and filming African Caribbean poets in London. I was successful with the application in 2000 and worked on my project alongside twenty-nine other (funded) young individuals with advanced skills in Media.

As part of the award scheme, I received training in Journalism, filming and editing from the BBC in London (White City site), received research experience at *The Daily Express* newspaper in Blackfriars, London and work experience on the longest running BBC children's programme called *Blue Peter* as well as work experience with other independent broadcasting companies in London. It was an amazing experience and was to prepare me for my future in community education through print media and local history. I received an award for my work from Chris Smith M.P, then Secretary of State for Culture.

to Hackney Council London, Department for Education, requesting financial support for further education. Thankfully, I was successful in my application and was offered a two-year, fully-funded maintenance grant and payment of college fees to attend the College of North East London between 1994 to 1996. I studied 'A' Levels in English and French and a City and Guilds Certificate in Radio and Print Journalism, gaining a Distinction.

I decided to write to Hackney Council, for a second time in 1996, explaining my success in my college studies they had originally funded and what I intended to do next. I formally requested financial help, through a second maintenance grant, to fund my higher education ambitions. Thankfully, Hackney Council's Education Department awarded me with a full grant for three years, allowing me to study for a Bachelor of Arts Degree in English with Theology and Religious Studies from 1996 to 1999 at St Mary's (Catholic) University College, Strawberry Hill Twickenham, on the outskirts of London.

Chris Smith MP presents award, 2000.   Photo: Nottingham News Centre

LEARNING TO LISTEN

A year into the new millennium saw a move towards working in the educational sector and a return to formal education on a part-time basis to advance knowledge in an understudied area of educational practice. In 2001, I found employment, through an advert in *The Guardian* newspaper, as a learning mentor in the Borough of Tower Hamlet, East London, mentoring pupils with barriers to learning such as a lack of motivation, poor school attendance or challenging behaviour. I was promoted to senior leaning mentor in 2002 until 2005 and studied, part-time during the evenings for a Master's Degree in Education at the Institute of Education, University of London (2001-2005).

By this point, I had spent most of my young adult life, almost eighteen years, in London and returned to Nottingham with my one year old daughter in November 2005, following the July 7th 'London Bombings'. I would have been caught up in the chaos of the bombings, as I would have been heading to work in Mile End, East London if I did not take advice from my mother to "come home" to Nottingham two days prior to this act of destruction and unnecessary loss of life. This experience made me realise the fragility of life and created a momentum of action in pursuing my literary and educational ambitions.

Once again, I returned to formal education and studied for a Post Graduate Certificate in Education (standard teaching qualification in the UK) in English from the University of Nottingham between 2009 and 2010 after working as a primary school learning mentor in Aspley, Nottingham from 2005. I completed my teacher training in English, which prepared me, to a degree, for teaching experiences in various secondary schools in Nottingham and county.

WRITE RIGHT: MY JOURNEY PUBLISHING AND EDUCATING IN THE COMMUNITY

Throughout my life's journey, I have found real joy reading literature, especially local history. I have a particular interest in local and global African Caribbean history as well as producing

Olivia O'Connor plays the violin for her school, 2012.
Photo: Nottingham News Centre

writing, in a journalistic way, about people who achieve or help others within the community.

In 2007, I researched and produced an exhibition about Black British Literature after receiving lottery funding to research autobiographies written by enslaved Africans (featured in the Nottingham Evening Post, October 2007). I wanted to lead this educational project in order to highlight the writing of Africans in Britain whose writings appeared in Britain (often published in London) from the mid-1750s onwards, that are under-studied and under-explored as credible and quality texts in literary history.

I am former Editor of Mojatu Magazine Nottingham and former Associate Editor of Mojatu Magazine Reading (2013-2014), community publications aimed at documenting community news and thus, improving the quality of life by giving people a voice, in Nottingham and beyond. (see.www.nottinghamnewscentre. com/magazines).

I have led the project to erect and unveil the first Blue Plaque (part of the Nubian Jak Blue Plaque Scheme) to a person of African descent in Nottingham. The George Africanus (c1763-1834) Blue Plaque will be situated at his former business residence and home on Victoria St, Nottingham.

I played a significant role in the Heritage Lottery funded project, educating the wider public about the life achievement of George Africanus and was part of the project's management steering group along with Rosanna Ottewell, the Project Coordinator.

I am currently Director of the Nottingham News Centre CIC, which sources and collates community news for websites, provides Journalism workshops as well as writing and editing services to organisations and individuals. I am part of the Nottingham Carnival Management Committee and a member of Antenna Media Centre, the Nottingham Local History Association (NLHA), the ACNA Centre, and work collaboratively on projects with the University of Nottingham (links with the Business School and their Institute for the Study of Slavery) and Nottingham Trent University (Community Outreach).

I am passionate about documenting local history and people who have significantly developed the community for the better, and hope, in the future, to support the researches and scripts for cultural publications and programmes aired on local and international television networks to better inform and educate the public. I have one beautiful daughter named Olivia.

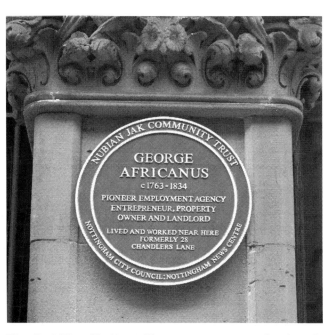

The first Blue Heritage Plaque to a person of colour in Nottingham, organised by Norma Gregory and team in 2014 for George Africanus, Entrepreneur.
Photo: Nottingham News Centre

GEORGE AFRICANUS BLUE HERITAGE PLAQUE
CEREMONY SPEECH

"Good afternoon everyone and thank you all for attending this very special occasion in the history of Nottingham: a Blue Heritage Plaque for George Africanus here, at his former residence and place of business in Nottingham and the first plaque for a person of colour in Nottingham.

It has been an honour and a privilege to host and sponsor this celebratory event, the first of many more, I hope for our community!

As a native of Nottingham myself of African-Caribbean descent, I believe, and have been witness to, massive progress and changes, over the years in Nottingham, towards being a city that is welcoming and inclusive for all nationalities, cultures, genders and age groups from all walks of life.

However, through the work of the late Len Garrison, George Leigh, Eric Irons, Leroy Wallace, Tony Robinson, George Powe and those living, namely, Des Wilson, Milton Crosdale, Lyn Gilzean, Merlita Bryan and many other community focused individuals, too many to name here, we thank them and dedicate this blue plaque for George Africanus, to all pioneers, in our community, from all walks of life.

George Africanus has inspired many people, younger and more senior, over many generations. His survival story and journey from West Africa, to Wolverhampton, then to reside in Nottingham in 1784, and HIS decision to pursue his professional and personal ambitions, by opening his own employment agency called Africanus's Register Office for Servants, despite hardships and setbacks, is a lesson of inspiration for us all.

I believe that George Africanus would be very proud and humble for this Blue Heritage Plaque tribute made today.

Finally, I would like to thank all the individuals and organisations that have contributed to this special event. I am truly grateful for the support and professionalism shared.

Much can be done with a combination of a vision, courage and a passion for celebrating achievement in the City of Nottingham.
Thank you!"

***

Speech given by Norma Gregory on behalf of the Nottingham News Centre, host and joint sponsor with Nottingham City Council of the George Africanus Blue Heritage Plaque Ceremony and Reception at his George Africanus's former residence and business premises, formerly 28 Chandlers Lane now the site of the Major Oak Pub, Victoria St, Nottingham, 9th October 2014.

Sharing history with the community: unveiling the George Africanus Blue Heritage Plaque on Victoria St, Nottingham 9th October 2014.   Photo: Nottingham News Centre

Ray Gale, a George Africanus researcher and historian.
Photo: Nottingham News Centre

GEORGE AFRICANUS

(c1763 -1834)

BLUE HERITAGE PLAQUE CEREMONY

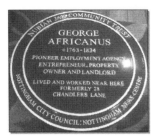

Thursday 9th October 2014

at

The Major Oak Pub, 11-13 Victoria St, Nottingham
(Formerly 28 Chandlers Lane in 18ᵗʰ/19ᵗʰ Century Nottingham)

Former Business Premises and Home of African Entrepreneur
George Africanus
Resident here, from c1788 until his death in 1834, aged 71.

WELCOME & INTRODUCTION

Jak Beula -Chief Executive
Nubian Jak Community Trust

Norma Gregory - Co Host and Joint Master of Ceremonies
Nottingham News Centre

3.00pm   CEREMONY SPEAKERS

Lord Mayor of Nottingham, Councillor Ian Malcolm

Nottingham City Council spokesperson
(Sponsor)

Nottingham News Centre spokesperson
(Sponsor)

PERFORMANCE TRIBUTE

By Miss Melissa Beason (Song 1)

BLUE PLAQUE UNVEILING

Guest Reception:
The Major Oak Pub, 11- 13 Victoria St Nottingham NG1 2EW

3.30pm   RECEPTION SPEAKERS
Thank You's / Reflections / The Future

3.45pm   Melissa Beason (Song 2)

3.50pm   REFRESHMENTS
Viewing of Images and displays

4.30pm   MEDIA CALL

4.45pm   GUEST DEPARTURES, DOORS OPEN TO PUBLIC
*(6.00 pm George Africanus Lottery Heritage Project,
Council House Civic Reception begins.)*

George Africanus Blue Heritage Plaque Ceremony Guest Brochure.

A Dedication and Thanksgiving Message

From Miss Norma Gregory M.A., Project Director
Sponsor, Nottingham News Centre CIC

Today we celebrate the life and work of George Africanus (c1763 - 1834), a native of Africa and citizen of Nottingham, through the honour of a Blue Heritage Plaque at the site of his former place of business and residence in the City of Nottingham.

When I think about the huge achievements and resilience of George Africanus, surviving enslavement from Sierra Leone in West Africa, probable transportation through Liverpool and on to Wolverhampton to work for the Molineux family, I think this is worth time to stop and reflect on what we have today and our opportunities to choose how we live our lives. George Africanus envisioned hope and moved to Nottingham, around 1784, establishing a successful employment agency business and provided employment and accommodation to others. He chose to marry and to raise a family as well as supporting the safety of others through his role in the 'Watch and Ward,' a voluntary policing service in 19ᵗʰ century Nottingham. He achieved much in his life through enterprise and community involvement.

I believe George Africanus would be proud of this honour today. Let us continue to celebrate his life by sharing his achievements with others, younger and senior, now and in years to come.

Kind regards as always,

Norma Gregory

Thank You!

Project Partners:

Many thanks to the volunteers and staff of the George Africanus Blue Plaque Project Partners. Their commitment, time and enthusiasm have been instrumental in the delivery of this project.

Designed by:
Catherine Joynson (cathy_mae@msn.com)

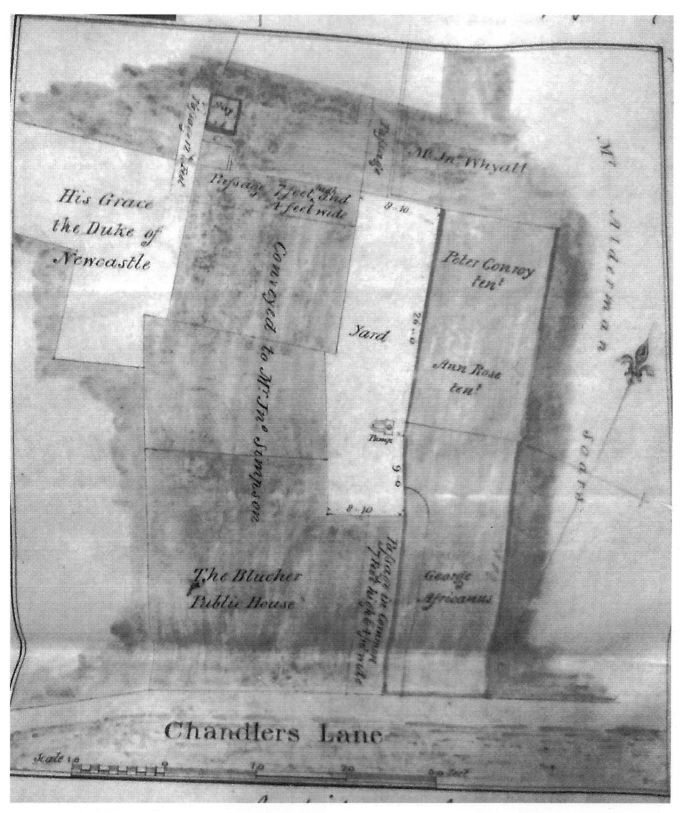

George Africanus's property deeds as recorded in 1829.

Courtesy of Nottinghamshire Archives.
Reference M/11044

CHAPTER 22

ARTICLES AND BOOKS BY NORMA GREGORY

BOOKS

Jamaicans in Nottingham: Narratives and Reflections (2015). Hansib Publications, London & Hertfordshire.

Slave Narratives of the Transatlantic Slave Trade (2007). Reference L02.2 held at Nottingham Central Library.

ACADEMIC JOURNAL ARTICLE (PAPER)

Gregory. N.J (2013) Deity, Distortion and Destruction: A Model of God in Alice Walker's The Color Purple. Published in *Black Theology: An International Journal*, Vol. 11, no.3, pages 363-372.

WRITINGS AS EDITOR AND SENIOR CONTENT WRITER, MOJATU MAGAZINES

Nottingham: Issue M009

Major Magnificent, Interview with the Lord Mayor of Nottingham.
Black Policing in Nottingham (news article).
Abdullahi Nur on a Mission for Olympic Gold (sports feature).
International Women's Day 2013 (news article).
Write Right! Proofreading (tutorial).

Nottingham: Issue M010

Interview articles with: Felix Cross, theatre director; Joseph Hall, dancer; Mellonie Page, singer.
Feature: 20 Facts and Stats about the Nottingham Carnival and Nottingham Carnival Archive,
Community news articles: Splendour Music Festival 2013.
Shiefton Supplementary School 30 Year Anniversary.
Write Right! Punctuation (tutorial).

Nottingham: Issue M011

Diva Divine: An interview with Eve Pitts, the first black Reverend Canon in the Church of England.
George Africanus 250th birthday!
Hard Talk: Interviews with BME Police Officers from Nottinghamshire Police Force.
Inklings of a Genius: Interview with Pitman Browne, Author, Performance Poet.
Article: Julius Garvey son of Marcus Garvey visits Nottingham.
Obituary: Oswald George Powe, Community Relations Pioneer.
Review: Senior Black Nursing Conference at Nottingham University.
Write Right! Capital Letters (tutorial).

Nottingham: Issue M012

Mic Check! Interviews with Black Female Journalists in Nottingham.
Article: Trent to Trenches: Nottingham Commemorates World War 1.
Article: George Africanus Lottery Heritage Project.
Article: Kenya Nottingham Welfare Association.
Write Right! Homophones (tutorial).

Reading: Issue R001

Write Right! Capital letters (tutorial).

Reading: Issue R002
    Mic Check: Interviews with Black
    Female Journalists
    Kenya Nottingham Welfare Association
    Write Right! Homophones

See http://nottinghamnewscentre.com/mojatu-magazine/

EDUCATIONAL RESOURCES

George Africanus: From Slavery to Freedom and Citizenship (2014). Consultant for schools educational activity pack created in collaboration with Nottingham City Council and Belong, Nottingham.

Text written for the George Africanus Calendar, 2015. Produced by Belong, Nottingham.

PRINT AND ONLINE MEDIA PUBLISHED WRITINGS

In depth research on early African narratives and their links to Britain. Online at: https://www.youtube.com/watch?v=v3MdwXGVYCI http://nottinghamnewscentre.com/normagregory/slave-narratives-research/

Newspaper article, The Methodist Recorder, p.6 'Ghana Fellowship Choir Perform in Nottingham' 10/05/13, Issue 8107.

News article posted on www.vibeghana.com about Ghana Methodist Choir performance in Nottingham

http://vibeghana.com/2013/04/29/ghana-methodist-fellowship-uk-chaplaincy-perform-at-mapperley-methodist-church- nottingham-england/

Nottingham Evening Post article and photo of visit made by Councillor Merlita Bryan, the first black female Sheriff of Nottingham, to the African Caribbean Centre (ANCA) Nottingham. Printed on the 4th August 2012.

Letter to The Teacher, a professional magazine for teachers. In the April-May 2010 edition. *'NQTs-Don't miss it!'* Review p.6 http://www.teachers.org.uk/files/Learning-Journal.pdf

Text/content for the George Africanus website: www.georgeafricanus.com

DISSERTATIONS

An exploration of whether primary learning mentor technique promotes effective learning. M.A. dissertation (2005) Institute of Education, University of London.

John Gabriel Stedman's 1796 Narrative and the Negro Experience engraved by William Blake (1757-1827). B.A. dissertation (1999) St Mary's College, University of Surrey.

CHAPTER 23

CONCLUSION: NEXT STEPS....

In bringing this collection of narratives and reflections from *Jamaicans in Nottingham*, let us hope that this text will be catalogued as a record of many Jamaicans in Nottingham who have reflected on their lives and their unique but collective journeys of achievements and challenges and thus, through the joys and hurdles of life, have helped to shape history in Nottingham.

Part and parcel of any author's triumph in biographical and autobiographical writing, is enmeshed in the attempt to capture the essence and vivid accounts of their subject before memories fade and vital information and images disappear forever through time. I thank those interviewed in this book, who have chosen to share their memories and reflections for future generations, so they may learn from these narratives and make an improved difference in the world. I hope that much can be learnt from this text, regarding motivation, wisdom and resilience.

I thank all of the contributors involved in this work and those who have allowed access to share their vision and dreams. For some, perhaps just sharing with the reader the joy and privilege of travelling on a boat for the first time, could be considered a great achievement.

There are many who perhaps did not get the chance to be interviewed for this publication due to time and space. Therefore and perhaps in the future, there will be more volumes to add to this edition, as there is much more to capture and preserve through oral history research.

To finish, I have included a poem written in 1989, that explores the notion of identity and the importance of being proud of who we are and our story. *Enjoy!*

SOUL FRUITION

Am I Jamaican?
Am I British?
Am I West Indian?
Am I Black?
Am I English?
Am I White?
Jamaican am I.
African I am...
I - West Indian? I.....
I am Indian? Could be...
English I am. Not!
White? Most definitely not
Black - as a dutch-pot.
So what?

Let me be ME!
Thank-YOU.

© Norma Gregory, 1989

Sunset in Montego Bay, Jamaica.

Photo: Nottingham News Centre

SECTION 3

JAMAICANS IN NOTTINGHAM

Additional Information

I

FURTHER READING

BELLE, C. (2002) St Kitts and Nevis Meadows Community: Memories for the Millennium. Nottinghamshire Living History Archive Millennium Award Scheme.

BLACK, C. (1958, 1998 Twelfth impression) History of Jamaica. Longman Publishers.

BROWN, D.A. (1997) Laying Up the Standard: Nottingham West Indies Combined Ex-Servicemen Association. Self-published.

BUTE, E.L. and HARMER, H.J.P. (1997) The Black Handbook: The People, History and Politics of Africa and the African Diaspora. Cassell, London.

BYGOTT, B.W. (1992) Black and British. Oxford University Press.

DABYDEEN, D., GILMORE, J. and JONES, C. (2007) The Oxford Companion to Black British History. Oxford University Press.

FRYER, P. (1984) Staying Power: The History of Black People in Britain. Pluto Press, London.

GILROY, P. (2007) Black Britain: A Photographic History. Saqi Books

MURRAY, R.N. (1996) Lest we Forget: The Experiences of World War II West Indian Ex-Service Personnel. Nottinghamshire West Indian Combined Ex-Services Association/Hansib Publishing.

PHILIPS, M. and PHILIPS, T. (1998) Windrush: The Irresistible Rise of Multi Racial Britain. Harper Collins, London

SEWELL, T. (1998) Keep on Moving: The Windrush Legacy, The Black Experience in Britain from 1948. Voice Enterprises LTD, London.

VAN SERTIMA, I. (1988, 1995, 3rd edition) Great Black Leaders: Ancient and Modern. Journal of African Civilizations LTD. Inc.

WILLIAMS, C. (1987) The Destruction of Black Civilization: Great issues of Race from 4500 B.C to 2000 A.D. Third World Press, Chicago, Illinois, USA.

II

ESSENTIAL WEBSITES

AFRICAN CARIBBEAN NATIONALS ARTISTIC CENTRE
www.acna.org.uk

ARCHIVES AND MUSEUM OF BLACK HERITAGE
www.aambh.org.uk

BLACK CULTURAL ARCHIVES
www.bcaheritage.org.uk

BLACK PRESENCE: ASIAN AND BLACK HISTORY IN BRITAIN, 1500-1850
www.nationalarchives.gov.uk/pathways/
blackhistory
www.100greatblackbritons.com

HANSIB PUBLICATIONS LIMITED
www.hansibpublications.com

JAMAICA HIGH COMMISSION
www.jhcuk.org

NATIONAL ARCHIVES CATALOGUE
www.nationalarchives.gov.uk/catalogue

NOTTINGHAM BLACK ARCHIVES
www.nottinghamblackarchives.org

NOTTINGHAM HERITAGE GATEWAY
www.nottsheritagegateway.org.uk/people/
blackcommunity.htm

NOTTINGHAMSHIRE ARCHIVES
www.nottinghamshire.gov.uk/archives

NOTTINGHAM NEWS CENTRE
www.nottinghamnewscentre.com

PITMAN BROWNE, KITABU-PET PUBLICATIONS
www.kitabu-pet.com, www.youtube.com/
pitmanbrowne

III

UK UNIVERSITIES WITH SELECTED SPECIALISM IN AFRICAN CARIBBEAN HISTORY

This is by no means a comprehensive or authoritative list but simply a starting point for further enquiry. A selection of specialist lecturers, senior lecturers and professors has been included for guidance but is not comprehensive. Check for updates with each institution listed.

NOTTINGHAM TRENT UNIVERSITY
www.ntu.ac.uk
    Centre for Postcolonial Studies

UNIVERSITY OF NOTTINGHAM
www.nottingham.ac.uk
    Department of History
    (Dr Sheryllynne Haggerty, Dr Celeste-Marie Bernier)
    Institute for the Study of Slavery (Dr Susanne Seymour, Professor Dick Geary)
    Department of English (Dr Abigail Ward)
    School of Social Sciences (Professor Cecile Wright, Honorary Professor of Sociology)

UNIVERSITY OF WARWICK
www.warwick.ac.uk
    Centre for Caribbean Studies
    (Dr Robert Beckford, Professor David Dabydeen, Dr Gad Heuman)

UNIVERSITY OF BIRMINGHAM
www.birmingham.ac.uk
    Centre of West African Studies (Dr Benedetta Rossi)

THE QUEEN'S FOUNDATION, BIRMINGHAM www.queens.ac.uk
    Black Theology (Dr Anthony Reddie)

UNIVERSITY OF YORK www.york.ac.uk

Department of History (Dr Henrice Altink, Professor James Walvin)
Centre for Eighteenth Centre Studies

UNIVERSITY OF HULL www.hull.ac.uk
    Wilberforce Institute for the Study of Slavery and Emancipation

UNIVERSITY OF DUNDEE www.dundee.ac.uk
    Transatlantic Studies

EDINBURGH UNIVERSITY www.cas.ed.ac.uk
    Centre of African Studies

GOLDSMITH COLLEGE, UNIVERSITY OF LONDON www.gold.ac.uk
    Centre for Caribbean Studies

SCHOOL OF ORIENTAL AND AFRICAN STUDIES (SOAS), UNIVERSITY OF LONDON
www.soas.ac.uk

QUEEN MARY AND WESTFIELD COLLEGE LONDON www.qmul.ac.uk
    Department of English

INSTITUTE OF COMMONWEALTH STUDIES www.commonwealth.sac.ac.uk

BRISTOL UNIVERSITY www.bris.ac.uk
    Department of Archaeology

LIVERPOOL UNIVERSITY www.liv.ac.uk
    School of History

IV

AN APPRECIATION AND SELECTION OF BOOKS AND PAPERS AUTHORED BY AFRICAN CARIBBEAN WRITERS FROM / IN NOTTINGHAM

Ancel P. Pennant
A little of Everything

Andrina Louis
Trailblazers

Andrina Louis and Donna Griffiths
Tracing the Trailblazers: A tribute to the early lives of Jamaicans in Nottingham through reminiscences. An education resource pack.

Black Ink Writers Group
Black History in Nottingham 'Respect Due'

Broxtowe African Caribbean Elders Group and the Association of Caribbean Families & Friends (ACFF)
A Walk Down Memory Lane

Carrol Rowe
Survivor: An Autobiography

Cecile Wright
Black Youth Matters: Transitions from school to success.

Christine Belle
St Kitts and Nevis Meadows Community: Memories for the Millennium.

Delroy Brown
Laying Up the Standard: Nottingham West Indies Combine Ex- Association. West Indian Ex-Service Personnel.

Errol Crosdale
Whom the Lord Loveth

Esther Goode
Mystery / Wonder and Intrigue

Glenda Agatha Nukporti
Triumph Over Pain

Icineth Spence
2001 Poetry Diary / Letter to the late 'Netty'

Lee Arbouin
The Nottingham Connection

Len Garrison
Beyond Babylon
The Black Presence in Nottingham

Lilieth 'Fay' Wade
Until Death Do Us Part

Lorna Holder
Moving Out: A Drama Project Exploring the Experiences of Caribbean Settlers in Industrial Nottingham during the 1960s.

Louise Garvey
The lives of Black Nurses Living in Nottingham

Madge Saunders
Echoes of a Whisper

Michelle 'Mother' Hubbard
The Irish Jamaican

Nezzle Saunders
Divine Inspiration

Norma Gregory
Deity, Distortion and Destruction: Model of

*God in Alice
Walker's The Color Purple. Black Theology:
An International Journal Vol 11 No.3 / Slave
Narratives of the Transatlantic Slave Trade,
2007 / Mojatu Magazine Nottingham, Issues
M009, M010, M011, M012 / Mojatu Magazine
Reading Issues R001, R002. Jamaicans in
Nottingham: Narratives and Reflections*

Panya Banjoko
*Bibi's Museum / Harri at the Castle
No Tears For Me My Mother*

Paul Ifayomi Grant
*Blue Skies for Africans / Buy Now Pay Later
/ Sankofa, the Wise Man and his Amazing
Friends*

Pitman Browne
*Inklings of a Black Christ / Wishing can be
Dangerous / Children get out of the Ghetto
Mentality / Community Writing / What is my
Mission?*

Robert Murray
*Lest We Forget: The Experiences of World War
II Servicemen*

Rosey Thomas Palmer
Hues of Blackness

V

JAMAICANS IN NOTTINGHAM:
A TIMELINE OF SIGNIFICANT EVENTS

1834

Number of enslaved Africans in Jamaica around 311,070. Compensation paid to British plantation owners in Jamaica, approximately £6,150,000.

1935

Marcus Garvey moves to Britain organises and directs the Universal Negro Improvement Association from London.

1940

10 June - Marcus Garvey dies in London.

1951

According to the 1951 UK Census, there was an estimated total of 2, 024 Jamaicans living in the UK.

1958

23 August -Nottingham Race Riots in St Ann's.

The Race Relations Board was set up following the 1958 Race Riots. Mr Eric Irons invited to liaise with the Race Relations Board and West Indians living in Nottingham.

10 September - Jamaican Premier, Norman Manley visits Nottingham following race riots.

Around 16,000 West Indians arrive in the UK, with around 2,500 West Indians moving to Nottingham.

1959

Mr Clifton Theodore Mitchell opens the first of many Caribbean food stores in Nottingham. The original shop was on Willoughby St, Lenton but was later demolished to build Willoughby Flats. Clifton Mitchell opened his second shop on Union Road, off Mansfield Road. He decided to close shop business for five years but still ran a mobile van selling Caribbean provisions. His next shop 'The Bowl' at 155 Ilkeston Road opened followed by another shop on Carlton Road called the 'G & N Store'. Since 1978, his son Colin Alexander Mitchell has continued to manage the family business now called 'Mitchell's Soul Food Store' at 175 Alfreton Road, Radford, Nottingham.

1962

10 April - Sir Alexander Bustamante becomes the first Prime Minister of Jamaica.

Conservative government passed the Commonwealth Immigrants Act 1962, which removed the automatic rights of citizens of British Commonwealth countries to migrate to the UK.

6 August - At midnight the National Stadium in Kingston, the Union Jack flag is lowered and in its place, the Jamaican flag is raised for the very first time signifying that Jamaica had become an independent nation.

Eric Irons becomes the first black Justice of the Peace (JP magistrate) in Nottingham.

Mr Wellesley Robinson and family form V Rocket Sound for the demand of 'blues' and house parties in Nottingham, Derby and the East Midlands from 1964. Valerie Robinson ('Lady V') still helps to run the family music/DJ business. 2014 marks V Rocket Sound's 50th anniversary and considered to be pioneers in Nottingham's sound system history.

1963

10 November - Marcus Garvey's body is returned to Jamaica following his death in London in 1940 and is re-buried in Heroes Park, Kingston.

1965

21 June - Dr Martin Luther King is presented with the Keys of the City of Kingston at a civic reception at the National Stadium in Kingston, Jamaica.

11 October - The 100th anniversary of the Morant Bay Rebellion in Jamaica is celebrated.

Hyson Green Flats, a concrete maze of lower ground and upper floor flats with inter connecting pathways, is built housing many West Indian families. It is later demolished in 1987.

1966

21 to 24 April - His Imperial Majesty Haile Selassie, Emperor of Ethiopia, arrives in Jamaica for a three-day state visit.

4 to 13 August - Jamaica hosts the 8th British Empire and Commonwealth Games.

1967

Nottingham West Indian Students' Association founded by Milton Crosdale, Horrace Mead, John Wray, Cecile Henry, Vena Case and others.

John Wray graduates from Clifton College for Teachers and is employed by Morley School in St Ann's Nottingham.

1968

Charles Washington moves to Nottingham from Georgia, USA supporting the organisation of many projects in Nottingham from the early 1970s. He helps to develop: The Black Star Independent Film Club, (from 1971) ACNA Centre (from 1976), Chroma Arts (1982), UKAIDI Community Link Project (1982) as well as 'Back A Yard' Radio station with Leroy Wallace (from 1979 to the late 1980s) and the East Midlands African Caribbean Arts (EMACA) in order to support African Caribbean arts in the city.

1973

May - The Jamaican Government announces free education in Jamaican secondary schools and for Jamaicans admitted to the University of the West Indies. This was a revolution in Jamaica's education system under Prime Minister Michael Manley.

Ainsley Deer (currently Dr Deer) takes up position as Teacher at his old school, Elliot Durham in Mapperley, Nottingham.

1974

Appointment of the first black Police Constable in Nottingham.

1975

October – Nanny of the Maroons and Samuel Sharpe declared National Heroes taking the number of National heroes to seven. Charles Square in Montego Bay re-named Sharpe Square in honour of the national hero.

1976

December - The West Indian Sports and Cavaliers' Sports and Social Club established.

1978

26 November - The African Caribbean National Artistic (ANCA) Centre officially opened.

1980

October - Edward Seaga becomes Jamaica's 5th Prime Minister.

1981

10 - 12 July - Nottingham riots in Radford and Hyson Green.

17 April -Robert Nesta (Bob) Marley is invested with the Order of Merit (O.M.).

11 May - Robert Nesta Marley dies of cancer in Miami, USA.

The West Indian Cavaliers create the Marcus Garvey Centre at the site of the former Raleigh Bicycles headquarters, Lenton.

1982

Lee Arbouin sets up the Steve Biko Saturday School Project, teaching English, Maths and African Contribution to World History.

1983

13 February - Her Majesty Elizabeth II and His Royal Highness the Duke of Edinburgh pay a state visit to Jamaica to open the Jamaican Parliament in the 21st Anniversary Year of Independence.

1984

The Gleaner Newspaper celebrates 150 years of publication.

1985

Milton Crosdale appointed as Director of Nottingham and Nottinghamshire Racial Equality Council.

1987

8 January -The ACNA Centre Nottingham is badly damaged by fire.

1988

12 September - Hurricane Gilbert devastates Jamaica, causing billions of dollars of damage.

Tuntum Housing Association established through the help of Tyrone Brown, Leroy Wallace, Arnold Wright, Harry Joshua, Junior Berrenga Forbes, Lorna Pennycook and Sharon Reilly among others. Tuntum provides homes for many families, particularly from the BME communities and elderly people in the city. It now offers sheltered housing (Lyn Gilzean Court) training, catering and student placements. Since 1994, Richard Renwick, MBE became Chief Executive of Tuntum; Chair of the Nottingham Carnival Management Committee (Tuntum have successfully managed and hosted the Nottingham Carnival for 15 years since 1999) and a director of the East Midlands Caribbean Carnival Arts Network (EMCCAN).

1991

4 July - Leroy Wallace dies aged 44. Leroy was a founder member of Tuntum Housing Association and was committed to the advancement and development of black people in the community.

24 July - Nelson Mandela visits Jamaica with his wife Winnie.

1992

Lee Arbouin becomes cultural advisor at the Sheffield Education Department and then promoted to the rank of Inspector at OFSTED.

1993

9 August - Pope John Paul II visits Jamaica.

Prime Minister Michael Manley addresses West Indians and the wider public at the Royal Albert Hall, Nottingham.

1994

Shiefton Supplementary Youth Group and Supplementary School opens in Radford to support and development African Caribbean youth education in Nottingham.

Victoria Morse (neé Vicky Case) of Nottingham voted in as Mayor of the Royal Borough of Greenwich.

1998

Jamaica's national football team, the Reggae Boyz, qualify for the World Cup in France.

2002

6 August - Jamaica celebrates 40 Years of Independence. A thanksgiving service is held at St Peter's Church, Nottingham.

2003

18 February - Len Garrison, the Jamaican community activist and archivist dies aged 59. He directed the African Caribbean Family and Friends (ACFF) Educational Cultural and Study Centre on Beaconsfield St, Nottingham and later became Director of the Black Cultural Archives in Brixton, London. Len helped to create the Black Presence on Nottingham Exhibition in 1993, held at the Nottingham Castle and helped to write its subsequent publication.

Edwin Maxwell becomes Chairman and a founding Director of the New Art Exchange (NAE) in Hyson Green. He played a pivotal and successful role in acquiring its £5.3 million building grant.

2004

September - Hurricane Ivan, the second biggest in history after Hurricane Katrina, pounds Jamaica.

2005

August - Hurricane Katrina devastates New Orleans, USA.

2007

National and local events to celebrate the Bicentenary of the Abolition of the African Slave Trade.

February – Kemet Radio directed by Mr Andrew Campbell, is launched as Nottingham's urban radio station.

15-21 October - Exhibition by Norma Gregory titled Slave Narratives, held at Nottingham Central Library produced through Lottery funding.

25 March - George Africanus (c1763-1834), African and Nottingham based entrepreneur, re-dedication of his grave and green plaque unveiling held at St Mary's Church Nottingham with Des Wilson.

3 July - Mr Eric George Irons, J.P, O.B.E and first West Indian appointed as a Magistrate dies aged 86. The funeral service was held at Our Lady of Perpetual Succour, Bulwell and included tributes from Des Wilson, George Leigh and a representative from the Jamaican High Commission.

2008

Jamaica experiences its best ever sporting performance at the Beijing Olympic Games with 6 gold, 3 silver and 2 bronze medals. Twenty-one year old Usain Bolt is elevated to superstar status winning the gold in the 100m, 200m and 4 X 100 m relay, breaking the world record on each occasion.

2010

24 January - Calvin 'George' Leigh, former manager of ACNA and Equal Rights Campaigner dies one day before his 80th birthday. His funeral is held at St Marys, Church, Nottingham. Tributes are given by Reverend James Stapleton, Mr Anderson, George Powe, Martin Gawith,

Bettina Wallace and Eddie Maxwell.

The Blue Mountain Women's Group is formed by Veronica Barnes, Jamaican researcher and historian.

2011

UK Census estimates around 22,000 people of Black Caribbean / African living in Nottingham, around 81,000 Black Caribbean / African living across the East Midlands and around 1.87 million people of African heritage in the UK.

2012

National and local celebrations for Jamaica's 50th Year of Independence.

5 August - Jamaica 50th Thanksgiving Service held at St Peter's Church, Nottingham.

6 August - The Jamaican Flag is raised in the Nottingham City Council House in recognition of Jamaican contribution in Nottingham.

August - The Honourable Usain Bolt wins gold medals in 100, 200 and 100 metres relay Olympic finals in London.

2013

30 March - Councillor Merlita Bryan becomes the first Jamaican, female Mayor of Nottingham.

27 April – Dr Martin Glynn is honoured at the New Art Exchange Nottingham through Nubian Link for completing his Doctoral studies in Criminology.

19 June - Nottingham News Centre, a community interest company is formed by Norma Gregory to help educate through Journalism, print and media production in Nottingham.

8 July - BME Experiences of Policing in Nottingham research report into African Caribbean people in Nottingham and their experiences of police 'Stop and Search' and other police practices by Professor Cecile Wright, completed and shared with Nottinghamshire Police and the general public.

9 September - George Powe, Secretary of ACNA Centre and long-standing management committee member and community pioneer dies.

28 September - Black Achieving Men Awards held at the Marcus Garvey Centre, Nottingham. Over 300 guests attended. Event hosted by Cllr Merlita Bryan and managed by Natasha Bryan.

4 October - Dr Julius Garvey, son of the late Marcus Garvey visits Nottingham. Garvey is honoured at the Nottingham Council House and speaks to students at Nottingham Trent University as well as the Jamaican community at the ACNA Centre, Nottingham.

2014

George Africanus: from Slave to Freedom and Citizenship a Lottery Heritage Project by Belong Nottingham, with Rosanna Ottewell as Project Coordinator, ends following training for 120 volunteers in creative writing and Journalism; archive training and research, the production of a website, school resource book and touring exhibition. The George Africanus legacy group continue to promote his life and work.

9 October - Norma Gregory leads to erect and sponsor the first Blue Heritage Plaque, in collaboration with Nubian Jak Community Trust, for a person of African descent in Nottingham dedicated to George Africanus (1763-1834). The blue plaque is unveiled at the business premises and home of George Africanus on Victoria St, formerly Chandlers Lane. He became a prosperous citizen of Nottingham through his original business called Africanus's Register Office of Servants.

2015

15 April - Book launch of *Jamaicans in Nottingham: Narrative and Reflections* at Fives Leaves Bookshop, Nottingham.

SECTION 4

JAMAICANS IN NOTTINGHAM

Photo Gallery

' In country' Jamaica 1930s.
Courtesy of Lena Gregory

George Leigh (left) and friends a night out at the Astoria Ballrooms, late 1950s.
Photo: courtesy of Kate Hayward

Mother and child, Nottingham 1960s.

Courtesy of Kate Hayward

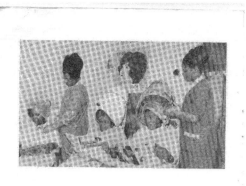

If you want to be noticed
why not try altering your appearance
by visiting

Joyce's Hair Fashions
26 RALEIGH STREET
Nottingham   Tel. 79505

24

Business advertisement, Nottingham 1960s.

Courtesy of Pitman Browne

REG'S PHOTO
Studio
PHOTOGRAPHER
for
PASSPORTS : PARTIES : PORTRAITS
PHYSIQUE : CHILDREN : WEDDINGS
295 ARKWRIGHT STREET
Nottingham

4

Business advertisement, Nottingham 1960s.

Courtesy of Pitman Browne

Then stop at
REO HAIR FASHIONS
for the Latest Hair Styles
Appointment not always needed

Specialist in—
Pressing   Styling   Colouring   Perming
and all other Beauty Cultures

Reo Hair Fashions
177 WOODBOROUGH RD., NOTTINGHAM
Telephone 53437

2

Business advertisement, Nottingham 1960s.

Courtesy of Pitman Browne

When shopping
call on us for your
West Indian
FOODS
WINES and **SPIRITS**
ALEC'S CONTINENTALS
141 WOODBOROUGH ROAD
Nottingham   Tel. 53791
30

Business advertisement, Nottingham 1960s.
Courtesy of Pitman Browne

Business advertisement, Nottingham 1960s.
Courtesy of Pitman Browne

Shiefton Youth Group & Supplementary School, Lenton Boulevard, Nottingham.   Photo: Nottingham News Centre.

Reverend James Stapleton.

Photo: Nottingham News Centre

Veronica Barnes, director of the Blue Mountain Women's Group, Nottingham.
Photo: Nottingham News Centre

Dr Martin Glynn, of Nottingham, Criminologist.
Photo: Nottingham News Centre

Mr Edwin Maxwell, Chairman of the New Art Exchange, Nottingham.
Photo: Nottingham News Centre

Mrs Carmelia Burke and Glenis Williams at the New Art Exchange. Photo: Nottingham News Centre

George Africanus beer in the making at Castle Rock Brewery, Norma Gregory with brewery staff, Gary Gibbens. Photo: courtesy of Castle Rock Brewery.

Dionne Rose, celebrity and music pioneer, Valerie Robinson of V Rocket Sound. Photo: Nottingham News Centre

KD Infinity, DJ at Kemet Radio Urban Station, Nottingham. Photo: Nottingham News Centre

Jamaicans in Nottingham, Independence Day celebrations, 2012.   Photo: courtesy of Michael Edwards.

Cllr Eunice Fay Campbell.   Courtesy of Nottingham City Council

Cllr Merlita Bryan.   Courtesy of Nottingham City Council

Cllr Marcia Watson.   Courtesy of Nottingham City Council

Tony Robinson, Sheriff of Nottingham, 1989-1990 and 1997-1998.   Courtesy of Pitman Browne

Alderman Hylton Beresford James.
Courtesy of Nottingham City Council

Desmond Wilson Lord Mayor of Nottingham 1993-1994, 2004-2005.   Courtesy of Nottingham City Council

George Africanus Heritage Lottery Project volunteers and Rosanna Ottewell (2nd from left) , Project Coordinator. Maria Teresa Tzelepaki (left), Madeleine Lee (right) Olivia O'Connor and Norma Gregory (middle).

Photo: Nottingham News Centre

Leslie Robinson, Nottingham Carnival management 2000-2010.

Photo: Nottingham News Centre

'Patti Dumplin' aka Lisa Jackson at work promoting better health in the community of Nottingham.

Photo: Nottingham News Centre

Calvin Wallace, Pam Bailey and Ralston 'Kojak' Taylor (right) celebrating Jamaica Independence August, 2014 at Mansfield Rd Baptist Church, Nottingham. Photo: Nottingham News Centre

Pastor E. George Beason. Photo: Nottingham News Centre

Rosey Palmer Thomas, Jamaican author.
Photo: Nottingham News Centre

Joe 'Rodney' James' of St Kitts, aged 20, a soldier in the British Army from 1970-1976. Photo: courtesy of Joe James

Gunner Joe James on tour in Detmold, Germany 1970. Photo: courtesy of Joe James

Joe 'Rodney' James, former soldier in the British Army who served in the 1970s Northern Ireland conflicts. St Kitts born and friend of the Jamaican and West Indian community for decades. Photo: Nottingham News Centre

Eric Mills of St Kitts, Band leader, Nottingham Carnival Club. Photo: Nottingham News Centre

Trevor Howell, Jamaican food businessman and creator of Miss Will's Pickles (left) with friends.

Photo: Nottingham News Centre

Dr Kevin Brown, Aerospace Engineer and Radio Broadcaster.

Photo: Nottingham News Centre

Christine Belle (St Kitts), playwright, author and radio broadcaster (Back-A-Yard and Kemet FM).

Photo: Nottingham News Centre

PHOTO GALLERY

Carrol Rowe, Jamaican author. Photo: Nottingham News Centre

Louise Garvey, historian and author of *Nursing Lives, Black Nurses of Nottingham* (2002).
Photo: Nottingham News Centre

Michael Walker, Jamaican Filmmaker and Lecturer.
Photo: Nottingham News Centre

Lisa Robinson, community campaigner and director of Bright Ideas, Nottingham.
Photo: Nottingham News Centre

125

New life, new lands – West Indians arriving in London.   Courtesy of Nottingham Journal newspaper

Mr. E. G. Irons, on whose right is the chairman of the city Education Committee, Councillor John Kenyon, interviews two mothers at the Shelton-street Infants' School, Nottingham, in the course of his inquiry into possibilities of further education for coloured adults in the city.—See Topics of the Day.

Mr Eric Irons at work: quest for equality and inclusion, 1960s.   Courtesy of Nottingham Evening News / Journal

He's a JP in 'race' city

New JP Mr. Eric Irons . . . "a great honour."

A JAMAICAN was appointed a magistrate yesterday—in a city where race riots flared four years ago.

He is believed to be Britain's first coloured J.P.

The new magistrate is 40-year-old Mr. Eric Irons, who lives with his English wife and their five children in a council house at Clifton, Nottingham.

He will serve on the Nottingham Bench.

In 1958 Mr. Irons was appointed an education officer to help Nottingham's coloured people after violent riots had swept the city.

Last night Mr. Irons said: "I'm deeply honoured. It has always been my aim to help the white and coloured communities to integrate.

"I am certain this is a step in the right direction and that other cities with big coloured populations will follow."

Alderman Cornelius Cameron, chairman of Nottingham Bench, said yesterday: "The Lord Chancellor always wants magistrates to be representative.

Population

"We have a big coloured population and the Bench ought to include a coloured magistrate.

"Mr. Irons is one of six new magistrates in Nottingham and will be sworn in next Tuesday.

IS he the first coloured magistrate?

A spokesman at the Lord Chancellor's office in London said:

"It is really impossible to say. Lord Chancellors have appointed magistrates for 600 years."

£1,000,000,000 is Neddy's big target

By LEN JACKSON, Mirror Industrial Reporter

BRITAIN'S "growth target" for the next five years should be to boost the goods and services we produce by £1,000,000,000 a year.

This was decided yesterday by "Neddy"—the National Economic Development Council set up by the Government to plan for future prosperity.

Growth

The suggested target represents an average rate of growth of 4 per cent, compared with a present rate of between two and three per cent.

An announcement by the council after its second meeting said sixteen industries are to be asked to give detailed information to see if this "reasonably ambitious" target can be met.

Nationalised industries to take part in the survey will include coal and electricity.

Private industries will include agriculture, chemicals, cars, petrol, wool textiles and chocolate and sugar confectionery.

The council's report on the survey should be ready by the end of the year.

'STOP THESE RED GANGSTERS' SOS

A call to the free world to help stop Communist "gangster" aggression in South Vietnam (South-East Asia) was made by Mr. Dean Rusk, America's Foreign Secretary, in Canberra, Australia, last night.

Earlier, it was announced that Australia was ready to send jungle fighting experts to join U.S. military advisers in South Vietnam.

WEATHER: Sunny spells, showers. OUTLOOK: Mainly dry.

SUNSET: Birmingham, 8.45; Bristol, 8.46; Derby, 8.43; Plymouth, 8.50; London, 8.36.

A man for all seasons: Mr Eric Irons, pioneering magistrate, 1962.

Courtesy of Nottingham Evening News / Nottingham Journal

A fine processional cross, chosen by Bishop P. J. Jones, Assistant Bishop of Sierra Leone, was given by Dr. and Mrs. Robert B. Wellesley Cole (right) as a gift to commemorate the 25th anniversary of St. Margaret's Church, Aspley, Nottingham. Bishop Jones is a brother-in-law of Dr. Wellesley Cole. The engraving on the cross is the work of Mr. J. Colley, a parishioner, and the cross was dedicated by the vicar, the Rev. C. H. B. Ridler (left), last night. Also in the picture are Mr. F. S. Clarke and Mr. H. H. Teather (churchwardens) and Mr. Richard Robinson (cross bearer)

Church procession in Nottingham, 1960s.   Courtesy of Nottingham Evening News / Nottingham Journal

THE NOTTINGHAMSHIRE GUARDIAN, SATURDAY, DECEMBER 28, 1957.   9

Calypso Carol?

The children of Nottingham's coloured community had their Christmas party just like their white cousins had, and there was a dusky Santa, too, with presents.   After their meal they had games, and Mr. J. W. Green led the carol singing.

Calypso Carol? Christmas party, 1957.   Courtesy of Nottinghamshire Guardian

man of the year.   for the best sports-

Clyde Walcott, who made 115 at Trent Bridge against Notts. on Saturday, signs autographs at the reception held for the West Indies team.

Members of the West Indian Cricket Team sign autographs. Clyde Leopold Walcott OBE, world class West Indian cricketer, Nottingham, 1957.

Courtesy Nottingham Evening News

Cynthia Baugh (12), who won the senior written poetry award in the Nottingham Poetry Society's competition, receives her certificate from Mr. Oscar Sewell. Looking on is Mr. Kennedy Williamson, the adjudicator.

Poetry winner, 1960s.   Courtesy of Nottinghamshire Evening News

The Rev. Arthur H. Bird entertains his young guests at a West Indian children's social evening held in the Bridgeway Hall, Nottingham, last night.

West Indian Children's Social Evening 1960s.   Courtesy of Nottingham Evening News

Teddy Boys' Warning: a news article following Nottingham's Race Riots, 26th August, 1958.

Courtesy of Nottingham Evening News

Norman Manley speaks at the Council House in Nottingham addressing the issues of discrimination and employment issues for migrants, 10th September 1958. Courtesy of Nottingham Evening News

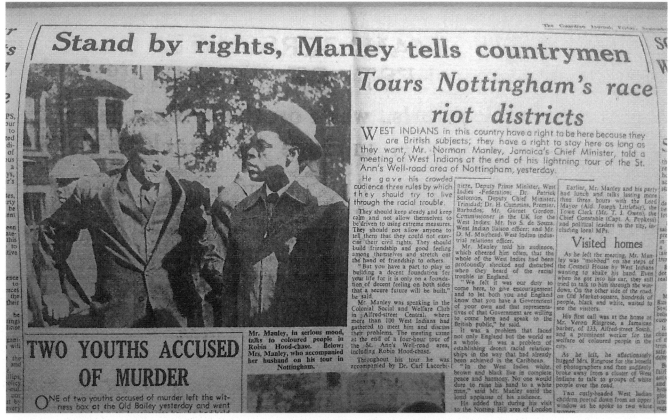

'Stand by rights, Manley tells countrymen', headline Friday 11th September 1958. As featured in the Nottingham Evening News.

Courtesy of Nottingham Evening News.

The Lord Mayor and Lady Mayoress of Nottingham, Coun. and Mrs. Oscar Watkinson, with the Jamaican High Commissioner, Mr. Ernest Peart (second from right), inspecting cultural exhibits at the opening of the Afro-Caribbean National Artistic Centre at the former Sycamore School, Hungerhill Road. Also pictured, from the left, are Mr. Sullay Jalloh, management committee member, Mr. Milton Crosdale, chairman, and Mr. George Powe, secretary.

Official opening of the ACNA Centre, November, 1978.

Courtesy of the Nottingham Evening Post

POSTPHOTO T4411/2

BRITAIN'S black youth face more employment and social problems than their white counterparts when they leave school, it was reported at a special careers convention in Nottingham.

The first-ever convention for young blacks was held at the Afro-Caribbean centre in Beaconsfield Road, Hyson Green.

It attracted pupils from five Nottingham schools after being opened by the Sheriff of Nottingham, Coun Tony Robinson.

A panel of black professionals, including solicitor Diana Frampong and doctor Chris Udenze, said the convention was arranged to give black youths more confidence in the employment market.

Organiser Ms Janet Burnett said that for years young blacks had been under-achieving at school.

"Success breeds confidence and hopefully the young people here today will go away with fewer worries about their future and job choices," said Ms Burnett.

'We want to get a message of hope over," she said.

The youths were entertained by Sneinton poet and writer Martin Glyn, who offered his own breed of rap poetry.

Martin, 31, of Edale Road, whose plays have been performed at the Playhouse and the Albert Hall, recently won a national young writers award.

He said: "We've all been through the system and we all know it's a lot tougher because of our skin colour."

●Mr Len Garrison (centre left), director of the Afro-Caribbean Families and Friends Educational Cultural and Study Centre in Beaconsfield Street, welcomes the Sheriff of Nottingham, Coun Tony Robinson, to the careers seminar. Some of the participants look on

Convention to support employment prospects for youth of African heritage held at ACFF, 1989.

Photo: Nottingham Evening Post

INDEX